ONE TOUGH
MOTHER

ONE TOUGH
MOTHER

SUCCESS IN LIFE, BUSINESS, AND APPLE PIES

GERT BOYLE WITH KERRY TYMCHUK
FOREWORD BY MARK O. HATFIELD

WestWinds Press®

WestWinds Press®
An imprint of Graphic Arts Center Publishing Company
P.O. Box 10306
Portland, OR 97296-0306
503/226-2402; www.gacpc.com

Fourth printing 2006

Library of Congress Cataloging-in-Publication Data
Boyle, Gert, 1920-
    One tough mother : success in life, business, and apple pies / by Gert Boyle.
        p. cm.
    ISBN 1-55868-908-7 (hardbound)
1. Boyle, Gert, 1920– 2. Columbia Sportswear—History. 3. Sport clothes
    industry—Oregon—History. 4. Businesspeople—Oregon—Biography.
    I. Title.
    HD9948.5.U62B69 2004
    338.7'68716—dc22   2004026486

President: Charles M. Hopkins
Associate Publisher: Douglas A. Pfeiffer
Editorial Staff: Jean Andrews, Kathy Howard, Jean Bond-Slaughter
Editor: Timothy W. Frew
Production Staff: Dick Owsiany, Susan Dupere
Design: Elizabeth Watson

Printed in the United States of America

Additional captions: Page 32: After fleeing their homeland my father and mother
never looked back, regarding themselves as Americans from the moment they
arrived in Oregon; Page 50: Tim, Kathy, Sally, and a family pet in 1963. I spent
most of that decade driving them around; Page 192: At the Albuquerque Balloon
Festival. Please refrain from making jokes about hot air.

DEDICATION

*This book is dedicated to all the employees
of Columbia Sportswear, past and present.
Your loyalty, creativity, and hard work have been the key
to our success. As I've told many of you before,
you will get your reward in heaven—and if you don't,
please let me know.*

*Proceeds from sales of this book will be divided between
Special Olympics and CASA for Children of Multnomah
and Washington Counties. For more information
about these outstanding organizations, please go to
specialolympics.org and casahelpskids.org.*

ACKNOWLEDGMENTS

Making a ski jacket is a team process and so, too, is making a product to put inside a book jacket. Among those who were part of the team that made this book a reality are: My children—Tim, Kathy, and Sally—who cheerfully provided their memories and who have always made this tough mother a very proud mother, as well; Many wonderful folks at Columbia Sportswear, including Emily Petterson, Barbara Cason, Peter Bragdon, Bob Masin, and Dan Hanson; Ross Eberman of Carpe Diem Books, who believed in this project and was one of its most eloquent advocates; Kirsten Leonard; The entire crew at Graphic Arts Center Publishing Company and WestWinds Press, including Tim Frew, Juli Warner, Elizabeth Watson, Doug Pfeiffer, Kathy Howard, and Susan Dupere.

And Kerry Tymchuk, who through the past year became more than my coauthor, he became my friend.

CONTENTS

FOREWORD

Ever since two gentlemen named Lewis and Clark arrived here nearly two centuries ago, Oregon has been a magnet for pioneers. Whether they came by covered wagon in the 1850s or by a station wagon in the 1970s, what many had in common was a tendency to think a little differently, to take risks, and to persevere through bad weather (of which there is a great deal in Oregon) and bad times.

I had the privilege of serving as governor of Oregon for eight years, and to represent Oregon in the United States Senate for thirty years. In the course of that time, I traveled to every community in the state, visited thousands of businesses, and talked to countless of our citizens. I was constantly amazed at the inspiring stories of modern-day pioneers. And there can be no doubt that the "mother of all pioneers" is my friend Gert Boyle.

Gert's story is one that encompasses many of the great themes of the twentieth century. The glories of freedom and democracy can be seen in her family's escape from the horrors of Hitler's Germany and their finding refuge and a new life on America's shores. The enduring strength of the free enterprise system can be seen in the history of Columbia Sportswear, which began as a small hat store, and which now is one of America's leading outerwear companies. The changing attitudes about the role of American women in the workplace is seen in Gert's struggle to gain acceptance when she became president of Columbia Sportswear in 1970, and her eventual status as one of Oregon's most respected and successful business leaders.

Gert may be short in physical height, but her courage, her common sense, her perseverance, and her business acumen made her tall enough to shatter all the doubts, misconceptions, and glass ceilings that stood in her way.

Back in the days of the original Oregon pioneers, neighbors would gather from miles around to participate in community "barn raisings." That spirit of neighbor helping neighbor is alive and well in the twenty-first century because of people like Gert. She is one of Oregon's most generous philanthropists, giving quietly to worthy causes both large and small.

Immigrant. Wife. Mother. Business leader. Advertising icon. Philanthropist. Pioneer. To these words, which all describe Gert Boyle, you can now add the word "author." One of the reasons I am so grateful to have Gert as my friend is her candor and honesty—a quality that was sometimes in short supply in Washington, D.C. Whenever I wanted to know how a vote I cast or a statement I made was playing in Oregon, all I had to do was ask Gert. She brings that same refreshing honesty in sharing the remarkable story of One Tough Mother. I know you will find her story as entertaining and inspiring as I did.

Since I began this foreword by writing about Lewis and Clark, I should end it by pointing out—as Gert likes to do—that if Lewis and Clark had been outfitted head to toe in Columbia Sportswear attire—they would have been so warm and comfortable they would never have left Oregon!

> *Mark O. Hatfield*
> Governor of Oregon 1959–1967
> United States Senator 1967–1997

PREFACE

More than three decades have passed since December 4, 1970, yet the events of that day are still remarkably fresh in my mind. It was a Friday, and I was looking forward to a weekend of spending time with family and friends and making sure our home was ready for the holidays. My husband, Neal, was preparing for another day at Columbia Sportswear, the small outerwear retail manufacturing business my father had founded in Portland, Oregon, in 1938, and where Neal had served as President since my father's death in 1964. Sally, our twelve-year-old daughter, was getting ready for school.

The morning routine came to an abrupt end when Neal told me that he was suffering chest pains that wouldn't go away. He was forty seven years old at the time, and the only health problem he had experienced in our twenty-two years of marriage was a persistent case of hay fever, which he used to his advantage to keep from ever mowing the lawn. Alarmed, I immediately called our family doctor, who advised me to take Neal to a nearby hospital.

I quickly helped Neal into the front passenger seat, put an obviously distraught Sally into the backseat, and headed out. We were just a few minutes out of the driveway when I glanced over and realized that my husband's condition was going from bad to worse. Instead of continuing to the hospital, I made the decision to drive to the local fire department, as I knew it was staffed with an emergency medical crew. I was there within minutes, but by the time we arrived, Neal was gone.

I spent the rest of the day in a near state of shock. After I called them with the news, our two other children—twenty-one-year-old son, Tim, and our nineteen-year-old daughter, Kathy—immediately returned from Eugene, Oregon, where they both attended college. When they arrived home a few hours later, our house was full of friends and neighbors offering sympathy and help. Employees of Columbia Sportswear were also there, stunned at the news of Neal's death, and uncertain as to what the future held for the business and their jobs.

Their concern was echoed by Neal's banker and his lawyer, who arrived to offer their condolences and to remind me of the fact that Neal had recently taken out a $150,000 loan from the Small Business Administration, pledging our house and my mother's house as collateral. For the past several years—indeed, for much of its history—Columbia Sportswear had operated as essentially a break-even proposition. Neal's business advisors were wondering if the loan payments would continue to be made on time. They questioned whether someone who had been a housewife and a mother for the past twenty-two years could run a business. They were not wrong to wonder; I was already asking myself those same questions.

After making funeral plans all weekend, I showed up for work at Columbia Sportswear on Monday morning, and I've been showing up ever since. Thanks to tenacity, creativity, the dedication of amazing employees, a few lucky breaks, and a brilliant advertising campaign that made millions believe I was the toughest mother in America, Columbia has done just fine, thank you.

Back in December of 1970, Columbia Sportswear was a family-owned business with forty employees, and annually sold about $800,000 worth of outdoor apparel to a clientele largely located in the Pacific Northwest. I am now the proud chairman of one of the world's largest outerwear brands and the leading seller of skiwear in the United States. Columbia is now publicly held and employs more than two thousand people around the world and distributes and sells products in more than sixty-three countries to more than 11,500 retailers internationally. And in 2004, our annual sales topped the $1 billion mark.

The success of Columbia Sportswear and twenty years of starring in our print and television advertisements have allowed me to achieve a certain degree of notoriety. As a result, I am often sought out by businessmen and women interested in the secrets of Columbia's success, as well as by individuals seeking guidance on how to persevere through personal setbacks and professional challenges. This book is an attempt to answer those questions and to share my story and Columbia's story, before I get too old to remember them. This is not one of those memoirs where someone recounts in great detail everything that ever happened to them in their life. I'm too busy to write that book—and I suspect you are too busy to read it. Rather, this book is just like me—short and to the point.

Age does have some advantages, one being that the older you get, the more leeway people give you to speak your mind. A forty-year-old who tells it like it is might be called blunt or abrasive but an eighty-year-old who does the same is termed candid or refreshing. In that spirit, what follows are my candid and refreshing memories on my first eighty years, and some thoughts on the lessons I learned along the way. I hope that those who find themselves facing circumstances they believe are beyond their control might find inspiration in the story of one tough mother and one great company.

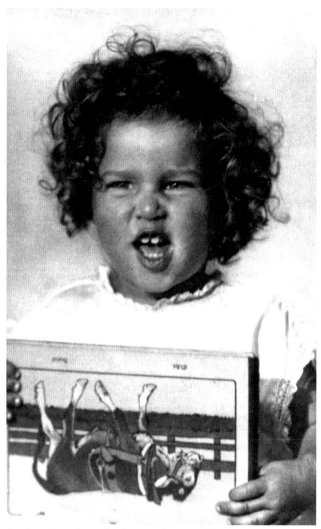

Here I am at age three, already expressing my opinions.

1

CHILDHOOD MEMORIES

I was blessed with the greatest gift that any child can have—the gift of loving parents. In my case, I had a father and mother who not only gave me life, but who saved it, as well, through their decision to flee our native Germany as Adolf Hitler's plans for Jews like us became clear.

I suppose that the clothing business has always been in my blood. My father, Paul Lamfrom, followed both his father and his grandfather into the clothing business, and achieved success as the owner of one of Germany's largest shirt factories. The factory and our home were in Augsburg, a city located in Germany's Bavarian region about forty miles north of Munich. Dad was one of Augsburg's most prominent citizens, respected for his business leadership and for serving with great distinction and courage in the German army during World War I—service that included spending a year as a prisoner of war.

In today's terms, Dad probably would have been called a workaholic. He went to the factory early each day and usually came home late. His work ethic would be one that inspired me when I found myself at the helm of Columbia Sportswear, and it is one that still guides me as I drive to the office each day. Dad liked to work, but he also liked to laugh—a trait I also share. He was very funny, and I treasured the time each evening when he would arrive home from the factory, as did my sisters: my older sister, Hildegarde, born in 1922, two years before me, and Eva, born in 1929. There was no doubt that Dad's three daughters had him wrapped around our collective little fingers.

Standing just over five feet tall, my mother, Marie Epstein Lamfrom, was proof that good things do come in small packages. Those who mistook her petite stature for weakness were in for a surprise. She had a spine of steel, which allowed her to persevere through some incredible hardships as a young woman. At age seventeen, when World War I broke out, she was sent by the German army to serve as a nurse on the Russian front—even though she had received no medical training whatsoever. Although she rarely discussed the horrors she witnessed there, she did tell me that keeping the rats away from the wounded soldiers and watching helplessly as a cholera outbreak claimed hundreds of victims were memories that would never leave her.

Though my father's financial success allowed her to preside over a spacious four-story house and to employ three maids, my mother never took money for granted. She closely watched our every expense, insisting, for example, that my sisters and I wear aprons and sleeve protectors over our dresses, so they would last longer. Much to the dismay of us three girls, who much preferred new clothes to hand-me-downs, the darn things worked. Hildegarde would wear a dress until she outgrew it, and then pass it down to me. In turn, I would wear it until it was too small and then pass it down to Eva. Once Eva had outgrown it, the dress would receive one more use, as it was cut into scraps to make clothes for our dolls. When people now ask me why my wardrobe still includes dresses that are twenty-five years old, I tell them I am hoping they might come back in style—but I also know that the acorn did not fall far from the tree, and that my mother's thriftiness lives on.

My earliest childhood memory is the time I was spanked for walking on our piano. My parents had told me not do it, but I did anyway. I guess I always was something of a rebel. I can also recall when I was told at the age of five that there was a special surprise awaiting me in the house. "Is it a chocolate bar?" I asked hopefully. It wasn't. It was Eva, my newborn baby sister. And I can still hear my Aunt Ida, who would take my sisters and me for walks in the park, during which she would describe in great detail the plot of the latest opera production she had seen. I had thought that some of *Grimm's Fairy Tales* were a bit on the scary side until I heard of the murders and tragedy that seemed to be part of every production. Seventy years later, I still can't bring myself to attend the opera.

The first four years of my formal education were spent in German public schools. I don't remember much of what I learned back then, but I do remember that the teachers were very strict. Writing German script is much different from writing English, and many of the letters have loops that are difficult for young children to form. Once, after making an error on a loop, my teacher brought me up in front of the classroom, had me put my hands out, and gave them several painful swats with a bamboo stick. Needless to say, I was more careful the next time.

When I reached fifth grade, my parents enrolled me in the Stetten Institute, a private all-girls school in Augsburg, which my mother had attended years before. Eventually, Jews were prohibited from attending the Institute, so my parents enrolled my sisters and me in a Catholic school. The nuns who taught the classes had no problem that my sisters and I were Jews in a Catholic school. They did have a problem, however, with the fact that I was not the same caliber of student as my older sister, Hildegarde, and they constantly urged me to study harder. (Always gifted with a brilliant mind, Hildegarde would later go on to a very successful career as a prominent research scientist.)

I did not share the same fascination with science and math that my sister did, but I always enjoyed the occasional visit to my father's business, where I was mesmerized by the sight and sound of hundreds of seamstresses working at their sewing machines. There were, of course, no labor unions or workers' rights in Germany at the time, and employees in many factories were little more than indentured servants. Dad, however, treated his employees with kindness and concern, and they were very loyal to him. He knew that loyalty wasn't earned simply by giving his employees a paycheck. It was earned by giving them respect. I learned at an early age that while one measure of a successful company, is, of course, the bottom line, another, and perhaps more important measure of success is how well the company treats its employees. If you are loyal to your employees and treat them with kindness, respect, and concern, you will earn that loyalty back tenfold.

If there was one thing that made Dad angry it was people who put on airs or considered themselves superior to others. "What they think they are, I've been for a long time," was a line he would mutter under his breath whenever he met someone who was a little too self-important. (And it's a line that I've muttered a time or two, as well.)

I exhibited at an early age some very definite ideas on fashion. My grandmother would often knit long underwear for us, and my mother expected my sisters and me to wear it, despite the fact that it made us itch like crazy. She never knew that when we walked to school, we would stop to take off this underwear and hide it in a nearby building. When school was over for the day, we stopped by the building to retrieve the underwear and slipped it back on before arriving home.

I was nine years old when Adolf Hitler came to power, and can still vividly recall the day he visited Augsburg. All the children were let out of school to run into the center of town to see him. People handed out flags with swastikas so that we could wave them as his motorcade drove by. Not knowing or comprehending the monstrous plans that Hitler was to implement, and caught up in all the excitement of the day, I was there with the other children, waving my flag and cheering, fascinated with the pomp and circumstance.

In a traditional German household, the children are protected from bad news. While my parents were very careful to hide their worries about the direction Germany was taking, the scope of Hitler's hatred of Jews was becoming increasingly obvious. Nazi officials arrived at our house on several occasions to ask questions of my father, and they wrote "Jews live here" on the outside wall of our house and on the sidewalk in front. Some of our friends stopped calling on us to play. We were also not allowed to shop in certain stores or to swim in the local pool. My sisters and I did not understand the reason for these changes, and our parents were reluctant to tell us the full story. With a smile, my mother simply told us that since we couldn't go swimming in the pool, we would instead go on a picnic in the park. My mother was determined for us to live a normal life, and to carry on with dignity, despite the awful reality of what was beginning to happen around us.

Thankfully, Dad foresaw what might happen if we remained in Germany, and although he loved his country and his business, he decided that our family had to leave as quickly as possible. He sailed to America in May of 1936 to finalize the plans for our move, first making his way to San Francisco to visit his mother, who had immigrated there years earlier, and then continuing on to Portland, Oregon, home to an older brother who had previously moved from Germany to America. The immigration laws of the time required someone to sign an affidavit vouching for you, and his brother provided Dad with the necessary papers, as well as the promise of a job in a hide company, owned by a cousin.

After his return to Augsburg in the summer of 1936, my father began the task of obtaining visas for our

Me at age twelve—one year before our move to America.

family—a process that often became a bureaucratic nightmare from which some would never escape. On one of his visits to the immigration bureau to check on the status of our paperwork, Dad had the good fortune to cross paths with a clerk who had served with him in World War I, and who remembered and admired his heroism. It wasn't long after that fortuitous meeting that news came of the approval of our paperwork. My father always believed that if not for that clerk, we might have been unable to make it out of Germany in time.

There were many other Jewish families of our acquaintance who, like my parents, decided to leave Germany. The Nazis made things more difficult through a policy that dictated that no Jew leaving the country could take with them more than the equivalent of twenty dollars in cash. This meant that my father would essentially have to give away the business he had worked so hard to make a success. Since we wouldn't have any money of our own with which to buy goods when we arrived in America, my parents chose to purchase as much as they could before we left. Our "luggage" for the trip to America included two containers the size of small rooms. Inside those containers were furniture, appliances, and clothes and shoes in a variety of sizes, which would fit my sisters and me for years to come.

Finally, in July of 1937, we rode the train to Hamburg, where we boarded the ship that would take us to our new life in America. I was thirteen years old, and while we were leaving relatives and friends behind, I was still very excited about what I thought of as a great adventure. The gravity of the situation from which we were escaping did not really dawn on me until years later. Tragically, some of our relatives did not fare as well. My grandmother—my mother's mother—did not attempt to leave until it was too late, and we later learned of her death in one of Hitler's concentration camps.

Looking back, it is hard to imagine the emotions that my parents must have felt at the time. My father and mother both risked their lives for their country in World War I. Yet that did not matter. They were being chased out of Germany for the simple fact that they were born Jewish. I know how fortunate I am. Because my father acted, and because he had the financial means necessary to emigrate, my parents, sisters, and I escaped the worst of the persecution, and did not meet the terrible fate that befell millions of Jews. It would take sixty years after leaving Germany for me to bring myself to return. After convincing me to join him on a business trip to Munich, my son Tim suggested we take the train to Augsburg. After arriving at the Augsburg station, we hailed a cab, and although my recollection of street names and directions was very sketchy, we somehow managed to find the way to my childhood home.

Later on that trip, a German reporter writing a story about Columbia Sportswear asked of my journey to Augsburg, and commented that seeing the house where I grew up must have brought back many warm memories. He was surprised when I responded, "I felt nothing." I continued, "Don't you remember history? The last time I was here, people were trying to kill my family."

2

A NEW COUNTRY: A NEW LIFE

My parents seemed to relax almost immediately upon boarding the ship. Although they did not know precisely what the future held for us in America, they knew we were safely beyond Hitler's reach.

My memories of the six-week trip that brought us to America include catching a glimpse of Don Budge, who had just won the 1937 Wimbledon tennis championship, and who boarded the ship at its first stop in Ireland; exploring every corner of the ship with my sisters; and seeing my parents dressed up in their evening wear for dinner. I suppose I would have had more memories if I had spent more time on deck and less time in our cabin battling seasickness.

For me—and I'm sure for untold thousands of immigrants—the most enduring moment of the passage from Europe was the first glimpse of the Statue of Liberty as we entered New York Harbor. What a magnificent sight it was! Over the years, our advertising and public relations folks have dressed me up in about every outfit imaginable, and they even suggested a time or two that I should pose as the Statue of Liberty. I have always refused, however, because for me—and for countless other immigrants who arrived at Ellis Island—the Statue of Liberty symbolizes the greatness of America. Putting on a crown and holding a torch might make for a good picture, but it would also be disrespectful. Take it from someone who should know: the Statue of Liberty is one great mother.

Dad originally hoped that we could travel from New York City to Portland by train, but unlike the passenger ship lines, the American railroads had no ability to sell tickets in foreign countries. Since we would have no cash with us when we arrived in New York, my father had to purchase tickets before leaving Germany that would take us our entire route—from Germany all the way to Portland, Oregon. So we remained on ship in New York, stopped briefly in Cuba, and then continued through the Panama Canal to San Francisco, where my father's mother provided the money necessary to buy train tickets for the final leg of our trip. After a short stay in San Francisco, we boarded a train north for the final leg of our trip. Our journey was completed on August 28, 1937, when we arrived in Portland.

The news printed in the Portland daily newspaper the *Oregonian* on the day of our arrival included an announcement that President Franklin D. Roosevelt would be making a trip to the west coast; a report that Italian dictator Benito Mussolini would soon be meeting with Hitler; and a photograph of the actor Humphrey Bogart, who was in Portland to view an amateur golf tournament. According to advertisements in the paper, pot roast was 19 cents a pound, bacon was 25 cents a package, and a 10-pound bag of sugar would have cost you 50 cents. For $795 you could buy a brand-new car.

Our first home was the Mallory Hotel in downtown Portland, where we stayed for several weeks until a house my father had rented was ready for us. My parents enrolled me in public school within days of our arrival, and since the only English I knew was the nursery rhyme "Hot Cross Buns," which the nuns had taught us in Augsburg, I was assigned to the first grade. Believe me; nothing motivates a thirteen-year-old to study quite like having a classroom full of six and seven-year-olds staring at you! It took just two weeks—with the help of my parents, who spoke fluent English, and who required from the moment we landed in America that only English be spoken in our house—until I was speaking my new language well enough to be advanced to the seventh grade.

Portlanders had not seen many German immigrants prior to our arrival, and as we rode the local streetcars, the long braids my sisters and I wore to our waist were often greeted with stares, pointing, and whispers. We also received more than our share of invitations to have lunch or dinner at the homes of neighbors who wanted a closer look at the "new kids on the block." One of these invitations nearly made me sick, though, when eggplant was included on the meal's menu. I had never eaten eggplant before, and one taste convinced me that I never wanted to eat it again. Wanting to make my mother proud of my manners and to make a good impression on our American hosts, I managed to eat all that had been put on my plate. Our hostess asked me if I would like some more, but as my English was not quite good enough for me to understand her question, I simply smiled and nodded. Much to my dismay, a second helping soon arrived on my plate. I have made it through my entire life without ever having a third helping. And I don't want anyone to send me any recipes with a note saying, "This doesn't taste like eggplant." I'm not going to eat the stuff, and that's final.

My family and I considered ourselves Americans and not Germans within weeks of our arrival. Part of this patriotic feeling might have been due to the fact that less than a month after arriving in Oregon, we got a glimpse of the President of the United States. President Roosevelt was in Oregon for the dedication of Timberline Lodge, located at the 6,600-foot level of Mount Hood, an hour or so drive from Portland. As he motored through the streets of Portland, the entire Lamfrom family cheered and shouted our approval. Even as a teen-ager, I could understand what a remarkable country it was when someone so new to America had the opportunity to see the President.

It took a little longer, however, to convince the government and some of our neighbors of our sympathies. When Germany invaded Poland in 1939 and war erupted in Europe, the government placed restrictions and curfews on German immigrant families. For a while, we were required to be in the house by 7:00 P.M. each night, and Dad was not able to leave the county on business trips until he received permission from the local district attorney. Dad took this in stride, seeing it as a small price to pay for the fact that our lives were no longer in danger. Even though restrictions were placed on the way we lived our lives, we knew that it was nothing like what we left behind in Germany.

A few months after arriving in Portland, Dad borrowed money from his mother to buy the Rosenfeld Hat Company—a small business that sold men's hats. This, of course, was at a time when wearing a hat was almost a requirement for American men.

His first executive decision was that customers might be wary of buying a product from a company with a foreign sounding name like "Rosenfeld." These days, businesses considering a change of name spend millions on research and surveys. My father simply opened the phone book, noticed that a lot of businesses took their name from the river that runs through Portland, and the Columbia Hat Company was born.

It was a very dramatic change for my father to go in a matter of months from owning a shirt factory that employed hundreds to being the sole proprietor of a small hat store. Rather than becoming depressed, however, Dad embraced his new circumstances and new challenges. My father taught me many lessons, but the one I relied on the most during the weeks and months following Neal's death was to devote my energies to looking ahead to the future rather than looking back at the past.

As all small business owners well know, running a small enterprise is more than an occupation, it is a way of life—and not just for the business owner, but for the owner's family, as well. While my mother, my sisters, and I rarely visited Dad's business in Germany, the situation was much different in Oregon. Along with running the household, my mother pitched in by keeping the company's books and by offering her opinion as to whether or not a particular hat would sell. I think she enjoyed the fact that she was now much more involved in my father's life than she was before.

My sisters and I were also enlisted, and weekends would usually find us at the store, putting hatboxes together. We would take these little stakes and nail them together to make crosses to protect the hatboxes from being crushed. I hated every minute of it, because for every nail you hit with the hammer, you hit your hand three times.

I was also expected to earn spending money of my own, and during the summer months I worked in the strawberry and bean fields that were a short drive from Portland. It was hot, dirty, and very tiring work, but it taught me the lesson I suppose my parents wanted it to teach me—that working in the family business wasn't so bad. Years later, I taught the same lesson to my three children by insisting that they also spend part of a summer working in the fields for local farmers.

As I entered my senior year at Portland's Grant High School, I was surrounded by friends who seemed to know not only what they were wearing every day for the next week, but who had already decided where they wanted to attend college, what sorority they would join, who they hoped to eventually marry. While I knew that my future included college—my parents would have it no other way—I had no idea where I wanted to go or what I wanted to do, and saw nothing wrong with that. I may have spent hours building boxes at Dad's store, but I wasn't about to be put into one. Instead of applying with my classmates to Oregon colleges, I set my sights on the University of Arizona. Why? In reality, it was little more than a whim. I had enjoyed the adventure of coming to America, and I guess I was ready for a new adventure— and attending a college where I wouldn't know a soul seemed to fit the bill. Besides, after a lifetime of living in rainy climates, I was ready for a little sunshine. I still enjoy the sun, but have come to appreciate the fact that without rain people wouldn't buy raincoats.

When my train to Tucson pulled out of Union Station in Portland in the fall of 1943, it was the first time I had ever been away from my family. I didn't have long to wait for those new sights and experiences I was so anxious for. Finding myself between trains for several hours in Los Angeles, I hopped in a cab and had the driver take me on a tour of Hollywood. Although I didn't see Clark Gable or Bette Davis, just the fact that I was on my own was exciting.

Arriving on campus, I found my room in the girls' dormitory, which would be my home for four years. I would end up receiving a degree in sociology—I had some vague plans about saving the world—but I confess that my social life usually received more of my attention than my academic life. There were several military airfields and facilities in or near Tucson, and many soldiers were receiving training at the university. As a result, there seemed to be ten boys on campus for every girl. I confess to not being upset about this ratio, as my dating life in Portland was limited by the fact that once 9:15 P.M. rolled around, Dad would tell any boy who might be visiting me that the last streetcar departed in fifteen minutes. This not-too-subtle hint was accompanied by a glare that would soon send any potential suitor on his way.

My children have long been embarrassed by the fact that I met their father under a table. Over the years, they have adopted a version of the story wherein I was looking for something I dropped and he volunteered to help me find it. A nice story, but not true. What really happened was that I was at a Sigma Nu fraternity party that featured a beachcomber theme, complete with sand on the floor and students attired in swimsuits—which were a lot less revealing back then. As usual, it was hot outside, and the cold alcoholic beverages at the party were plentiful and hard to resist—so I didn't. I ended up under the table because I was having problems standing up. Their father was there because he was in the same condition.

Had I been in better shape then, I probably would have remembered later just what was said under that table. All I know is that I learned that his name was Neal, and that he made me laugh—although in the state I was in, I probably would have laughed at anything. Before leaving the party to make my way to my dorm, Neal asked if he could see me again. I accepted, and during our next few dates I learned that Neal had spent most of his life in Pennsylvania, moving to Arizona with his family in hopes of finding weather more hospitable to his mother's arthritis. He was gregarious, funny (even when I was sober), and 100 percent Irish-Catholic. It wasn't quite love at first sight, but it also didn't take me long to know that I couldn't imagine spending my life with anyone else.

In those days, some people couldn't imagine a Catholic and a Jew getting married, but Neal and I weren't among them. We knew we loved each other, and since I had

The newlyweds in Arizona.

attended a Catholic school for a number of years in Germany, I had a head start on the instruction classes, which I completed before Neal and I were married in Portland in the summer of 1948. We returned to Tucson in the fall so Neal could finish his degree.

Family planning was a foreign term in the 1940s, and Tim was born thirteen months after our wedding. Tim was a little reluctant to make his entrance into the world, so the hospital—hoping to speed things up—sent Neal and an extremely pregnant and very uncomfortable me on a bumpy Jeep trip through the Arizona desert. The expedition did the trick, and we made it back to the hospital in time for Tim to be born a few hours later.

Expenses were tight for our young family, and along with attending classes, Neal earned extra money by selling vacuum cleaners. A born salesman, Neal would often close the deal by telling customers that he would repair his product if any problems occurred. The only issue was that he had no idea how to perform this repair! To remedy the situation, Neal bought an old vacuum at an auction, and he and I spent our evenings taking it apart and putting it back together, learning in the process more than I ever wanted to know about vacuums, but learning, as well, that knowing a product and selling a product go hand-in-hand. It is a lesson I have kept in mind, and

Here I am with six-year-old Tim. Is that dress straight out of *I Love Lucy* or what?

47

while I don't expect Columbia's sales staff to be able to take apart and put together every piece of clothing we make . . . well, maybe that is what I expect.

My father liked Neal from the moment they met, and joked that after raising three daughters, he finally had someone with whom he could share a bathroom. After Neal received his diploma, Dad offered him a job at the Columbia Hat Company. I suspect the job offer also had something to do with ensuring that he could see his new grandson on a regular basis. It didn't take long to pack up Tim and everything we owned—which wasn't much— and head north.

3

A NOT SO DESPERATE HOUSEWIFE

From our return to Oregon in 1949 until Neal's death over twenty years later, my life was devoted to taking care of my husband and my family. Kathy was born in 1951, nineteen months after Tim, and Sally completed our crew in 1958. Truth be told, I loved every minute of being a wife and a mother.

As I look back on it, it seems that ours was a family straight out of a 1950s situation comedy, where the father worked all day, the mother raised the kids and took care of the home, and the highlight of the day occurred when everyone gathered around the dinner table. One thing my kids will tell you is that at our dinner table, the conversation was much better than the meal. In fact, they divided my recipes into two categories: brown things and green things. One of the brown things was round steak, which was my stand-by, and which I judged to be fully cooked when flames shot out of our wall-mounted oven. On an occasion when the kids were impressed by a mother of one of their friends who actually made a pizza, I tried to duplicate her culinary skills. I clearly did something wrong. Tim took a look at my masterpiece and assumed that one of his sisters had thrown up on the dinner table.

I may not have been much of a cook, but I was a great chauffeur. I was a soccer mom before anyone played soccer, as I drove one, two, or all three of the kids to and from school, a friend's house, or one of their many activities. After one particular day when it seemed that I never left the car, I pronounced to the kids my conclusion that when I died, I was going to spend eternity driving between Heaven and Hell.

Speaking of which, many summers we would load everyone in the station wagon and head to Tucson to see Neal's family. Needless to say, driving through the oppressive summer heat of Arizona in a car without air-conditioning might not strike everyone as a relaxing vacation, but Neal had a way of making everything enjoyable.

As the kids reached school age, they were enrolled in a local parochial school. My kids were the only ones at the school with a Jewish mother, and many of the nuns never quite knew what to make of me.

Their confusion turned to alarm one afternoon when I met Kathy after school and she broke down in tears as we were driving home. For the past several days she and others in her class had been having problems with a classmate who had been elected as a student leader. Kathy had told us the night before that this girl was inspecting the lunch trays of younger students, and would whack their hands if their milk was in the wrong place on the tray. Neal suggested that Kathy and the other classmates who objected to this behavior might want to sign a petition, asking that the student leader be removed from lunchroom duty. They did just that, and when the girl said her feelings were hurt, the nuns not only decided that Kathy should be punished, but for some reason they also instructed her that she couldn't tell her parents she was in trouble.

Kathy told me her story as we were driving home anyway, and I slammed on the brakes, did a U-turn, and drove back to school. I marched into the classroom and told whomever would listen that they should never tell a child to keep secrets from their parents. From then on, the nuns treated me with a mixture of fear and grudging respect. A friend suggested that I should just take charge of the school, proclaim myself the first Jewish nun, and call myself "Mother Shapiro."

Like other full-time moms, I also managed to squeeze in time for some volunteer activities. I was involved in parent-teacher organizations, and in the League of Women Voters. Any chance I might have had to become involved in local politics was lost when our Airedale terrier took a romantic interest in a prize poodle owned by the mayor of West Linn, who happened to live down the street. More than once, the mayor caught our dog trying to find a way into his yard, where he could continue his courtship of the canine femme fatale. The mayor threatened me with arrest if his poodle ever gave birth to puppies that looked suspiciously like an Airedale.

One thing I learned in running a household, which also came in handy when running a business, was how to pinch pennies. I became the neighborhood expert in finding bargains, many of which I discovered when I happened by the local Union Pacific rail station and discovered that they sold furniture that had been damaged in transit. I bought an oak table there for five dollars sometime in the late 1960s, and it still looks pretty good.

By the way, I discovered a few years ago that one thing I valued over thriftiness was pleasing Columbia's customers. While on a trip to the Oregon coast, I stopped to shop at a boutique that included Columbia products in its inventory. I saw a hat I liked—not a Columbia hat—and took it up to the counter, expecting to pay the eight-dollar price that I thought was marked on the price tag. When the storeowner rang up the sale, I learned that the price tag said eighty dollars and not eight dollars. Every bone in my spendthrift body wanted to explain the mistake and put the hat back, but since I was buying from a customer, I bit the bullet and paid for the hat. I also bit the bullet and started using reading glasses, which until then, I had been too vain to wear.

While we weren't by any means rich, Neal and I felt very fortunate. We had each other, three happy and healthy children, and wonderful friends. Moreover, Neal and my father had proven to be a good match. Dad was the "nuts and bolts" guy who knew how to make the trains run on time, and Neal was the visionary—the persuasive salesman who always seemed to know what the customers wanted.

As hats began to lose their popularity, Neal and Dad looked for other ways in which to expand the business. Noting the popularity of outdoor activities such as hunting, fishing, and skiing in Oregon and the Pacific Northwest, they started to sell a small number of outerwear products, including skiwear. When they were unsatisfied with a vendor from whom they were purchasing ski gloves, they decided to manufacture their own, establishing Columbia Manufacturing Company in 1959. One year later they merged Columbia Manufacturing and Columbia Hat into Columbia Sportswear.

Like most women of my era, I had been taught to sew as a child, and found the skill handy when it came to keeping my kids in clothes. I never considered myself much of a seamstress, however, and wouldn't have dreamed that I would play a role in creating the product that would mark the first real success of Columbia Sportswear.

That is just what happened when Neal came home one day and said that customers had been asking when Columbia would make a fishing vest with enough pockets to store their flies, pliers, line, and other necessities. Neal wondered if I could sew one that would meet their demands. Over the course of the next several weeks, I spent many hours at the sewing machine, as Neal and Columbia salesmen dropped by to inspect my progress, and offer suggestions. Since I had never fished a day in my life, their suggestions were quite helpful.

I added a magnet to the outside of the vest when someone said they didn't like digging in their pockets to find flies and lures. Frustrations with trying to hold on your fishing rod while simultaneously tying flies led me to attach a curtain hook that would hold the fishing rod and free up both of the angler's hands. When Neal showed the finished prototype to his customers, he knew from their positive reaction that he had a success on his hands. Columbia Sportswear's real seamstresses were soon working overtime, and sales of the vest played an important role in the slow growth of the company. It also taught Neal a lesson that was passed down to Tim and me, and that has remained at the core of the Columbia philosophy: We don't conduct product research in a design ivory tower or laboratory. We simply talk to our customers about what they want to buy, and we make it.

My father and Neal didn't have to look far to gain inspiration for other products for their business to produce; they simply glanced out their window. In Oregon it rains—a lot. Not surprisingly, it wasn't long before Columbia added rain gear for hunting and fishing to its product line.

I'm often asked by owners of small businesses how they can become owners of large businesses, and my answer is that you have to do it one step at a time. You have to crawl before you can walk. The expansion into manufacturing led to the hiring of a handful of new employees. The success of the fishing vest and rain gear allowed Columbia to take a few more steps forward. My father and Neal purchased a new building and hired additional sales staff and seamstresses. It was still a small enough business with twenty or so employees, $300–400 thousand in annual sales, and a shaky enough year-end balance sheet that required the whole family to pitch in. It was Tim's job to help clean up the new building, which had previously been home to a maraschino cherry canning operation. He swears that it took him years to wash away the odor of the cherries. All three of our kids were models in Columbia's first product catalogs.

My father passed away in 1964 after suffering a stroke. I know America isn't perfect, but when I hear someone harshly criticize our country, I am always tempted to tell them about my father's life. Few countries welcomed Jewish immigrants and their families in the 1930s, and fewer still offered the opportunities that America and Oregon offered Dad—the opportunity to buy and grow a business. I have wondered a time or two what Dad would think if he could see that the small wholesale hat business he bought in 1938 is now one of the world's largest and most successful outerwear companies. Whatever success Columbia Sportswear has achieved over the years is due in no small part to the standards he set and the values of hard work and honesty that he instilled in his family.

Upon Dad's death, Neal, then thirty-eight years old, became president of Columbia Sportswear, and his already busy workload increased—as did the workload of my mother. In the years preceding Dad's passing, Mom had become more and more involved in the daily operations of the business, where her duties included record keeping of the piecework being completed by the seamstresses. After Dad's death, Mom had no intention of becoming a widow who simply sat in her home or played bridge with the ladies, so she came to the office every day. She set an example I would later follow when she began to sign all the company's expense checks, running her frugal eye over each payment, making sure that every penny spent was spent wisely. It was a talent that was still very much needed. Neal was a more aggressive businessman than my father. He saw a great future for Columbia and was willing to spend money to achieve that future. More salesmen were hired and more products were manufactured. While annual sales slowly grew under Neal's leadership—eventually reaching $800,000, it was still a struggle to show a profit at the end of the year.

With all three kids now in school, I found more time to occasionally drop by the business. My visits were largely limited to talking to Neal and Mom, and greeting a few of the employees, each of whom knew more about what was going on at Columbia than I did—a situation that remained the same until December 1970.

Tim and me at the company in 1971. Keeping the business open was a day-to-day struggle.

4

SWIMMING AGAINST THE TIDE

If someone asked me to swim a mile, I would tell them I couldn't. But if someone took me out on a boat and pushed me into the ocean a mile from shore, you better believe I would start swimming. I guess that's what Tim and I did in the days and weeks after Neal's death. We started swimming, hoping against hope that we could keep our heads above water.

I don't recall actually asking Tim to come to work with me. He and I both knew instinctively that I needed his help. He had married just a month before Neal's death, with only a semester remaining until he would obtain his degree at the University of Oregon, and was planning a career in law or journalism. After Neal's death, without hesitation, he put his plans on hold.

The first thing we did when we went to the office on Monday, December 7, 1970—just three days after Neal's death—was to bring together all forty employees. I stood in front of them on the factory floor and tried to put on the most optimistic front I could, telling them that everything would continue as it was before, except that I would now be running the business. I told them that I couldn't do it by myself, and that I needed their help. It was a very emotional day and I surprised myself by getting all the way through my remarks without tears.

I don't know what I expected to happen once my speech was finished, but if I thought that everyone would hurry to their desk or sewing machine and get to work, I was mistaken. Instead, employees lined up to ask Tim and me for additional directions. It seemed that Neal's management style was to talk with each employee every morning and assign them their task for the day. They expected me to do the same; the problem was I didn't know what I was doing, let alone what they should be doing.

If ignorance is bliss, then Tim and I were the most blissful people on earth those first weeks, because we had absolutely no clue what was going on. We searched Neal's desk, hoping to find a document that would provide some guidance on the day-to-day operations of the business, but only found a few notes that made no sense. Some employees realized our predicament and offered suggestions about what needed to be done. Some others, however, chose to take advantage of our inexperience.

One of the first tasks we faced as the end of the year approached was to conduct an inventory of supplies and equipment. I had never performed an inventory before and was uncertain how to begin. A bookkeeper in the accounting department came to me and said she knew the inventory process and would be happy to take the lead, but there was one catch: she would only do it if her salary was raised from $900 to $1500 a month.

I didn't know if she deserved the raise or if the company could afford it, but my options were limited, since the inventory had to be done. What she forgot, however, was that women have memories. After she completed the inventory, I allowed her to stay at the company for another month and a half, and she then became the first person I ever fired. I knew that if Columbia were to survive, I needed to be able to trust our employees. And I couldn't trust anyone who was so quick to put their own personal interest above the interest of the business.

I have often compared those first months in charge of Columbia to Alfred Hitchcock's famous movie *The Birds*. Everywhere I turned, it seemed a new problem or crisis was pecking at me. Tim and I spent much of our first months in charge trying to convince our suppliers that the company was in good hands. Apparently, we weren't too convincing, as supplier after supplier canceled their deliveries, certain that the rumor circulating through the industry that we would soon be unable to pay our bills was true. It was a Catch-22 situation. If we were to pay our bills, then we needed to make money, but we couldn't make money if we weren't sold the material we needed to make products. In hindsight, I suppose the suppliers were being careful and making a smart business decision, but at the time it seemed that no one was willing to give us a chance. It would not be until several years later, when Columbia's survival was assured, that some suppliers finally began to give us a break, and provide us with needed materials without payment up front. I never forgot, however, who was willing to take a chance on us, and the businesses that cut us some slack during tough times are businesses we deal with still.

Adding to the pressure was the fact that I was feeling the guilt familiar to working mothers. I had a twelve-year-old daughter at home who had just lost her father, and now her mother was spending most of her waking hours trying to salvage the family business. I juggled as best I could, trying to find the time in each busy day to make the half hour drive from the office to school to pick up Sally and to ensure that she wasn't home alone.

Were there times in those first few months when I shed tears? You bet. But I learned from my parents that when circumstances around you change you can't stay home and cry all day long. Just as my father knew four decades earlier that if he wanted to save his family's life he couldn't sit around and wring his hands, I knew I didn't have time to ask myself if I was enjoying what I was doing or whether or not Columbia was going to survive. All I knew was that it *had* to survive, and I would do whatever it took to make sure it did. I could not forfeit on the SBA loan and give up my house and my mother's house, which Neal had pledged as collateral. Telling my mother that she had to move out of the house she had lived in for thirty years was a nightmare that kept me from sleeping for several nights.

As the days went by, I also found myself wanting to succeed for non financial reasons, as well. The more people that doubted me, the more I wanted to prove them wrong. There was a time or two when I couldn't help but feel like I was back as a thirteen-year-old first-grade student. All eyes were on me, wondering what I was doing there and doubting my abilities. It didn't take me long to realize that my challenge was made more imposing by the fact that I was a woman in an industry almost totally dominated by male executives. Several bankers suggested that in order for Columbia to survive, I needed to put a man in charge. I had paid little attention to the women's lib movement when I was a full-time housewife and mother, and while I wasn't quite ready to burn my bra (which would have created a three-alarm fire), I did believe that individuals should be judged by their ability rather than gender. I was also finding that some of the skills I had learned as a mother and in running a household were very transferable to the workplace—skills like urging people to get along with each other, and not spending money unless you have it.

These skills, however, didn't appear to be doing me much good, as by the end of 1971, Tim and I had managed to take a company with $800,000 in annual sales and turn it into a company with $600,000 in annual sales. Our bankers took a look at the precarious financial situation of the company, and correctly concluded that if we continued on that path, we would soon be broke. They called us in, said they were going to withdraw our line of credit, and told us that while we had given it our best, it was time to sell Columbia Sportswear.

I am many things, but a quitter is not one of them. Accepting the bank's recommendation to sell the company my father had founded and my husband had helped to build was the most difficult decision I have ever made. While my heart wanted to stay and fight, my head told me that our bankers were right. Tim and I were also physically and emotionally exhausted—tired of each other, tired of the pressures, and tired of days that never seemed to bring any victories.

I concluded that after selling the company I would have enough money left to tide Sally and me over for a while before I would have to hunt for another job. Since my work experience from the past twenty-plus years consisted entirely of running a company into the ground,

I had no idea what I would do to make a living, but thought I might survive by working as a clerk at Meier & Frank, a local department store. I never dreamed that someday Meier & Frank would be just one of many department stores that would sell Columbia Sportswear products.

Once the word got out that Columbia was for sale, a local business executive with apparel industry experience made what the bank thought was a reasonable purchase offer. Tim and I had some initial discussions with the executive and, nearing a final agreement, met again a few weeks later in our office for what we thought was the signing of some final documents. We were stunned when he went through the contract and began to pick it apart, line by line.

"Well, Mrs. Boyle," he said, "I really don't want your entire zipper inventory, so we will need to reduce the purchase price by that amount." "Here's another problem," he added, "I don't want to buy the entire building, so we need to make an allowance for that." He also declared that he wanted me to sign a "non-competition" clause, prohibiting me from working in the outerwear industry for a number of years. Since I had just proved myself as a failure at business, I suggested that he should require me to go to work for one of his competitors. He failed to recognize the humor in my suggestion.

By the time he was through listing his newly discovered objections I calculated that I would walk away from the sale with a grand total of $1,400. I may have proven in the past year that I didn't know much about business, but I damn well knew that Columbia Sportswear was worth more than that.

Perhaps he thought I was so desperate that I would sell at any price. Perhaps he thought he could take advantage of a woman. In either case, he thought wrong. All the frustrations that had been welling up inside me for the past year and a half bubbled over. I had learned a swearword or two during my life, and I used every one of them to tell him very graphically what I thought of him and just where he could put his offer. "For 1,400 dollars,

I would just as soon as run this business into the ground myself!" I yelled, before pointing to the door and telling him to leave.

I never saw the man again, and for many years could not even bring myself to say his name. As I look back on it, however, I owe him a great deal. Had he not tried to nickel and dime us at the last minute, had he simply signed the agreement we had previously reached, then I would have sold Columbia Sportswear, and the past thirty-three years of my life would have been completely different. I would have missed out on the opportunity to build a great company, to work with fabulous people, and to have gained faith in my abilities.

Our little company has grown pretty well over the years by engineering serious outerwear for serious outdoorsmen and women.

So when we decided to enter the skiwear market, our president (that's her to the right) handed down an edict. She's good at edicts.

I don't remember it word for word, but the gist of it was, Columbia is not going into the skiwear business with just another line of fancypants skiwear. We'd need something more technical, more advanced than anything out there.

Now, after considerable effort, we've done it.

"MY MOTHER REFUSES TO SELL A SINGLE PARKA TO SKIERS." *–Tim Boyle*

The Bugaboo! System™ of skiwear.

Far more than a collection of nicely coordinated garments, this is an entire new approach to wardrobing a skier. Through an ingenious zipper design, a number of parkas, jackets and vests can be worn by themselves or coupled together, as one. To cope with the wide swings in temperature from the lift lines to the lodge lounge.

There's a tough new outercloth called Bergundtäl™ that repels moisture and wind alike. And a Jægør Fleece™ that warms, insulates and resists pilling.

Certain models feature our patented new Radial Sleeve™ design that affords skiers a freedom of arm movement basically never before possible in a truly warm jacket.

Altogether there are five items in the system. For men and women. And, thanks to our exclusive Columbia Interchange System™ the Bugaboo parka and vests can also be coupled with some eight other unique Columbia outerwear garments. So if you're due for new skiwear this season, take a little motherly advice. Don't buy a single thing. Buy a system. Start looking for the Bugaboos!

Bugaboo Parka™ comes with zip-out Jægør Fleece™ liner. Wear either piece alone or both together for extreme weather.

Gaitors and pants are of Bergundtäl™ Cloth and both reversible for varied looks.

Vest is reversible and can be worn solo or zipped into parka.

BUGABOO!

◆ Columbia Sportswear Company

For a color brochure send $1 to us at 6600 N. Baltimore, Dept. P3, Portland, Oregon 97203.

5

TURNING
IT AROUND

I was still the same person the morning after I changed my mind about selling Columbia Sportswear as I was the day before, and the challenges my company faced to survive and succeed in a very competitive marketplace were just as steep. I was, however, more determined than ever to succeed. I wanted to prove to my detractors and to myself that I knew what I was doing. I received the opportunity to do just that when our bankers—perhaps impressed by my gumption in telling off our prospective buyer—agreed to extend our credit line for another six months.

Six months wasn't much time to prove that Tim and I had learned something during our first rocky year, so we moved quickly. First, we took a tough but necessary step when we fired some of Columbia's longtime employees. It had become clear to me that we had some very talented individuals who worked for us, and it had become equally clear that we had some who were much less talented. With the exception of the woman who used my inexperience with the inventory process to secure a raise, I had been very reluctant to let anyone go since Neal's passing. I thought that if they hadn't had any abilities, then Neal wouldn't have hired them. While I knew that Neal was gone and that Columbia was my responsibility, I was reluctant to act on my own intuition. I now had a second chance to keep Columbia afloat, and knew that unless changes were made, there wouldn't be a third opportunity.

Don't let Donald Trump fool you. Telling someone "you're fired" is not fun and is not something that will win you any popularity contests. There are times, however, when it is necessary. In our case, cleaning house allowed me to immediately reduce expenses at a time when every penny counted, and it allowed me to look for new employees who had talents and skills we needed to survive.

Tim and I also realized that up to this point we had been reluctant to ask for advice. In fact, it is now easy to see that we developed a bunker mentality in that first year, trusting only each other. The problem was that we not only didn't know what we were doing, but that we also didn't know that we didn't know. Tim recalled an observation that Neal often made: "Self-examination is better than self-defense." Our six-month reprieve offered a chance for self-examination and for examination by others who were smarter and more experienced than we had had the opportunity to be.

One of our bankers mentioned that he had recently loaned some money to a businessman who had impressed him with his abilities and experience. He suggested we recruit that businessman and others whom we respected, to serve on an informal board of advisors who could take a look at Columbia's operations and offer some frank advice.

Even though we couldn't offer these advisors anything more than our thanks, there were five or so businessmen—some of whom had known and liked Neal, others who perhaps felt sorry for a widow and her son—who agreed to offer us free advice. One of the first suggestions the group offered was that Columbia was making too many products. Given that there were many other better-known manufacturers in the clothing industry making products similar to ours, they urged us to focus on products that were unique to our company. Our sales catalog was soon trimmed from fifty-six pages to twelve as hundreds of products were dropped, and our related expenses were trimmed, as well. This was tough medicine to swallow. Again, it seemed that by eliminating products both Dad and Neal had added, we were somehow questioning their judgment and abilities. Eventually it dawned on me that above all, Dad and Neal would want the business they loved so much to survive—and if that meant reversing course or going in a new direction, then so be it.

Our informal board also suggested that we should not be ashamed to manufacture products that would bear the name of another company. Since my father and

Neal had moved the business from strictly sales into manufacturing, Columbia had made products for sale only under our name. That changed, and we secured some contracts to manufacture products that would bear the labels of well-known outerwear companies such as Lands End, Eddie Bauer, and Orvis. Although we have long since returned to manufacturing products only under the Columbia Sportswear brand, the income we made from these contracts helped to ensure our survival.

Nothing succeeds in business like success, and as our doors continued to stay open, the suppliers who had initially been slow to do business with a company they believed was headed for bankruptcy were no longer so reluctant. Just to be on the safe side, I would sometimes order twice as much of all the supplies we needed: our cash position was still on the shaky side and I thought that if our suppliers found out, they would once again cancel their shipments.

I knew we had turned a corner when our business increased to the point that we needed to put our employees on a double shift. I believed it was important for the employees to see that Tim and I were working just as hard as they were, so we would take turns working with the night crew. My daughter Kathy said she knew I was working too hard and too late when I became excited about finding a lawnmower with a headlight, enabling me to mow the lawn when I arrived home after dark.

One of the key factors of success in the outerwear and sporting goods business is the tradeshow circuit. There are a number of annual industry conventions where the buyers for the major retailers meet to personally inspect the products of the manufacturers. A good show resulted in a large number of orders that could make a company's year. Neal had excelled at these shows, and I knew how important they were to Columbia's future, but determined very early on that I should not attend. There were a number of reasons behind this decision. First, the shows were largely a man's world, and my presence there would have made some uncomfortable. Second, I knew that Tim was Columbia's future, and that he needed to be seen at these shows. The last thing he needed was his mother trailing after him, giving him advice in front of the people who needed to see him as a peer.

Still in his early twenties, Tim was quickly proving himself to be a gifted businessman, but some in the industry were as skeptical of his abilities as they were of mine. The generosity of one man helped to change that. One of the most respected individuals in the industry at that time was Harold Hirsch of Portland-based White Stag Company. Harold took a liking to Tim and made a point of spending time with him at the shows. Others in the industry would see the two of them together and assumed that if Harold liked him, then Tim must be okay.

When our six-month probation was over, I was able to return to the bank with increased sales numbers and reduced expenses. In turn, they agreed to extend our line of credit. One of my many meetings with the bankers provided them with something I'm sure they still talk about. Wanting to make a good impression, I put on my very best dress, and carried my raincoat—which I had just taken out of the dryer—over my arms. After our meeting, I returned to the office, and as I hung up my coat, I discovered to my horror that attached via static electricity to the back of my coat were a number of pairs of my underwear. It took me a couple of years before I could get up the nerve to ask my banker if he had noticed my fashion faux pas, and apologize if he had. He told me that he remembered that meeting—and my underwear—very well, but that no apology was necessary. "In fact," he said, "I felt a little bit sorry for you, which may have helped me decide to give you the loan."

We used the additional borrowing authority to purchase more equipment, as we needed to expand our capacity to keep up with increased orders. I would like to think that Tim's and my leadership was the reason that Columbia had turned a corner, but a good share of the credit was due to the fact that we were in the right place at the right time. Business schools can teach you many things but they can't teach good luck and timing.

In the 1970s, people were changing the way they dressed and the way they thought. Gray slacks and navy blue blazers were no longer the required uniform for the office. Americans were becoming more casual, and the clothes they wore for play were becoming more and more acceptable to wear at work. Those fortunate to live in the Pacific Northwest were also continuing their love affair with the outdoors. Nike—another Oregon-based company—took off in the 1970s as the jogging craze swept the nation, and, thankfully for us, the number of people hunting, fishing, and hiking seemed to increase every year. May it always be so.

By 1977, Columbia's picture had brightened considerably. We were approaching annual sales of $1.5 million. We had paid off the SBA loan in its entirety, and we paid off the mortgage on the company's building. Columbia was up to nearly sixty employees. And much to my surprise, I was selected by the Small Business Administration as the Small Business Person of the Year for Oregon.

Sally was now in college, so I was able to work even

longer hours, as I had no one who was waiting for me at home. Some of my friends were urging me to get a social life, and offered to fix me up with friends of theirs. I thanked them for their offer, but declined. I joke that in the decade or so following Neal's death, I was working so hard that I never had time to date, and once I became the center of our advertisements, no man wanted to date someone who was portrayed as being so mean and nasty. The fact of the matter is that I have never been interested in marrying again. Once you experience perfection, why settle for anything less?

As Columbia continued to grow, it became clear that the manufacturing department housed in our company headquarters could no longer keep up with the demand. Tim proposed that we follow in the footsteps of many of our competitors and open a manufacturing facility in Asia, believing that the cost savings that came with such a facility would help our bottom line. I was wary of doing this, as I was concerned that we wouldn't be able to exert enough control over a facility that was on the other side of the world. I also thought that having the "Made in America" label was much more preferable than one stating "Made in China."

As we had done many times before, and as we have done many times since, Tim and I discussed the issue in our usual manner. I told him what I thought and he told me what he thought—sometimes in loud voices. We listened to each other, and we challenged each other with questions. I came to the conclusion that on this issue, Tim was right. If Columbia was to continue to grow, then we had to be able to price our products competitively. The cost savings we would receive from opening a facility in Asia were substantial, and would allow us to manufacture and sell products at a price that was attractive to the consumer.

Still, I think we might have pulled the plug on opening a manufacturing facility in Asia if it hadn't been for Don Santarufo. Don had been a key part of our sales team for years, and he made the success of our Asia operation a one-man mission, living there for months, and personally training new employees—employees who he insisted would ultimately be placed in charge of the facility. We now have offices or facilities in twelve foreign countries, and foreign sales now comprise 35 to 40 percent of our business. One constant is that our operation in Germany is run by a German citizen, our facility in Sri Lanka is under the supervision of a Sri Lankan, and so on. Many other companies send an employee from the American headquarters to run operations in foreign countries. Tim and I have found that no one understands what works in a country better than someone who is from that country and has made it their home.

Our Asian facility was up and running in 1983, just in time to play an important part in the success of the first product to really put Columbia Sportswear on the map; a jacket with the unlikely name of Bugaboo.

For some time, Columbia had been making a hunting jacket that included a weatherproof outer shell, and an insulating fleece liner that could be unzipped and removed, according to the weather. Other retailers had begun to make similar jackets for skiwear and regular outdoor wear. We decided that we should enter the market. Our design team came up with a great-looking jacket, one that featured brighter colors than anything on the market, and that was also available in colors that might appeal more to women. Our competitors were pricing similar jackets in the \$250–\$300 range. We worked hard to keep manufacturing prices down without compromising quality, thereby allowing us to price our jacket at \$100. Tim also came up with the idea of naming the jacket after some of his favorite mountains—the Bugaboos in British Columbia. Our advertising agency urged us to reconsider the name, as they thought that customers would associate the word "bugaboo" with an error, and no one would want to buy a jacket that was a mistake. They recommended that some more customer research was necessary to determine a name that would help ensure strong sales. I reminded Tim that his grandfather had chosen the company's name out of the phonebook, so he should feel free to stick to his guns. He did, and the Bugaboo jacket was an instant hit.

One of the reasons the Bugaboo was so successful—and that other Columbia products have achieved strong sales—is Tim's and my philosophy that if you are going to make clothes, then you might as well try to sell them to as wide an audience as possible. I know this sounds obvious,

My mother came to the company every day until just a few weeks before she passed away. She taught me many lessons that guide me still.

but for a time it was akin to a revolutionary idea in the outdoor wear industry. The majority of our competitors were selling their products only to stores specializing in hunting or skiing products and patronized by committed outdoors enthusiasts. They considered it beneath them to have their products seen in large department stores such as J. C. Penney's or Sears. We had no such qualms. Sure, we wanted customers who would wear our products into the woods. But we also wanted customers who would wear our products to work, or for running errands on the weekends. We understood that only 20 percent of the outdoor apparel sold annually in the United States is used regularly for the type of sport the clothes were designed for. The other 80 percent is sold to people who like the rugged outdoor look but who don't plan on scaling a mountain anytime soon.

Selling our product to a large number of retailers also allowed us to keep our prices below our competitors, which led to increased sales. Our formula of selling a great product at a fair price to as many people as possible kept Columbia growing through the recession of the late 1970s and early 1980s, a time when many of our competitors were in economic trouble. As Tim pointed out, "Maybe in times that are terrific, people can buy a Prada purse that costs $1,900. But if they can get a Columbia backpack for $19.95, it's much more functional, and they still know and trust the brand."

I will always be grateful for the fact that my mother lived to see Columbia begin to have a name that was familiar and respected. Mom was diagnosed with cancer in 1982, and she continued to show up for work each day and play a vital role in the company until just a few weeks before her death in 1983 at the age of eighty-six. Mom not only kept working well into her eighties, but also continued to serve as the leader of a Portland Girl Scout troop—a position she held for forty-five years. From her days as a nurse on the front lines of World War I, to leaving Germany a step ahead of Hitler's grasp, to raising three daughters in a new country, to becoming a true partner in her husband's business, Mom experienced many changes in her long life, and she provided me with an example of how to take the punches life sometimes offers and how to stay on your feet until the final bell sounds.

6

EARLY TO BED
EARLY TO RISE
WORK LIKE HELL
AND ADVERTISE

By 1984, Columbia Sportswear's sales were approaching ten million dollars annually, and there was no question that we would survive. Tim and I had guided the company through some very tough times, and we had learned a great deal in our fourteen years at the helm. We did not always agree, and there was a time or two when we were very frustrated with each other. As anyone in a family business knows, it is not easy working with relatives. In fact, if you spoke to your employees like you speak to your relatives, you probably wouldn't have many people who wanted to work for you. You know the Achilles' heel of your relatives, and when tempers flare, you aim for it. Tim and I may have known each other's weaknesses, and we may have occasionally raised our voices at one another—but we also knew each other's strengths, and somehow we managed to juggle our relationships as business partners and as mother and son without ruining either. I guess Tim and I finally concluded that nepotism isn't all bad—as long as you keep it in the family.

I should add that my daughters Kathy and Sally have also had the pleasure—and the pressure—of working with their mother. Before leaving the company to devote herself full-time to motherhood and a wide variety of interests—including successful ventures in commercial real estate and the arts—Kathy ran a number of our company outlet stores in Central Oregon. Sally worked for a number of years in our Portland headquarters, where she managed our retail operations. Like her grandfather did nearly seven decades before her, Sally also bought a business of her own—Moonstruck Chocolates, a manufacturer of gourmet chocolates—and now operates that company from the same building where Columbia was headquartered for many years. As someone who has long had a sweet tooth, having a daughter who owns a chocolate company is about as close to heaven as you can get!

Tim and I had no idea in 1984 that our mother-son relationship would soon be the focus of an advertising phenomenon that would propel Columbia Sportswear into two decades of remarkable growth and which would turn this short, gray-haired grandmother into something of an international sex symbol.

Columbia's first attempts at advertising were a bit primitive. There was an elderly German man who worked for my dad in the early days of the Columbia Hat Company who would feed the pigeons that roosted near the office. Eventually, the birds grew to trust him to the point where they would allow him to pick them up. While he had them in his grasp he would quickly paste Columbia Hat stickers under their wings and, when released, the birds would serve as a flying billboard. I always thought this was a risky strategy, as I was sure that one of the pigeons would release a special delivery that would strike someone down below.

By the 1980s our ads were a little more traditional. Prior to 1984, Columbia Sportswear's print advertisements had featured the equivalent of blueprints of our products. The text in the ads highlighted how the various product features would keep those wearing it warm and dry. At the bottom of the ads was our tagline: "We don't just design it. We engineer it." The ads were designed to appeal to the outdoorsman who was looking for a sturdy and reliable product. They were similar in tone and in theme to our largest competitors. They were also a tad bit boring.

Left to our own devices, Tim and I probably would have plodded along with that advertising campaign for several more years. Thankfully, however, we were blessed with the advertising agency of Borders Perrin Norrander. The name partners of that agency—Bill Borders, Wes Perrin, and Mark Norrander—had been thinking of how they could differentiate Columbia from our competitors, and give us our own unique identity. The sporting goods industry is one that then and now is dominated by men. And Bill, Wes, and Mark concluded that the one fact that really made Columbia different was that I was the president. They came to Tim and me and told us that they wanted to take our ads in a different direction. Blueprints and boasts of engineering were out; I was in. I would be portrayed as the world's most exacting boss—a tough mother—who demanded and expected nothing less than the best out of my son and my company, personally inspecting each and every product we manufactured.

I wish I could say that at the moment they proposed the new advertising campaign a lightbulb went off in my head, and I shouted "Eureka!" The fact of the matter was that I was initially skeptical. After all, from the day of Neal's death until then, I had dealt with vendors and customers who did not believe a woman could or should run a company. I could still hear the businessman, who, upon learning that I was president of the company, proclaimed,

"But you're a woman." My response to him? "You know, I noticed that when I got up this morning." Humor aside, I was concerned that in an industry with the vast majority of products being sold to men, the presence of a little old lady in the advertisements would be a liability rather than an asset. And let's face it. I have never been accused of looking like a supermodel. If we were to have a woman in our ads—why not someone who our male customers would respond to?

Before a final decision was made, I agreed that we should follow the practice that had worked for us in the past: listening to our customers. Tim and I shared the proposed advertising campaign with a few of our most trusted and reliable customers and asked for their honest reaction. The verdict was a unanimous thumbs-up: they thought the ads were funny and memorable. Based on that response, Tim and I agreed we should give the new campaign a try. It was the best decision we ever made.

The impact of the ads was almost instantaneous. Sales quickly increased, and I was surprised when strangers came up to me on the street and asked if I was the "tough mother." Better yet, the image created by the advertisements took hold. Instead of seeing us as just another outerwear company, our customers thought of us as the company where the cranky and crotchety old broad made sure that they were getting a good product at a fair price. The bottom line was that what we were really expressing was that we were human. Think about when you deal with a utility company or some banks these days. You never talk to a human being: you always talk to a machine. Our ads set us apart from the corporate pack. People relate to us because they believe there is a person at Columbia who really cares. And the best thing about our ads is that they are true. I do care.

While I may not have been smart enough to predict the success of the ads when they were first shown to me, I was smart enough to know that we should keep a good thing going. I have remained at the center of our print and television advertisements for the past two decades, and the folks at Borders Perrin Norrander have teamed with our in-house public relations and marketing experts to portray me as tougher and sassier with each successive year. The recognition and smiles I received wherever I went after the print advertisements began increased ten- and twentyfold once we started to advertise on television. Our first broadcast commercial featured me forcing poor Tim to walk through a car wash to prove the durability of our outerwear. It was an instant hit, and other commercials where I push Tim around have followed.

Not coincidentally, Columbia Sportswear sales have increased each successive year since the tough-mother advertising campaign began. The increased sales are not due solely to our advertising. No ad, no matter how creative, can make up for a lousy product. What our advertisements continue to do, however, is to convince customers to try our products—and once they do that, then we've got them for life.

Twenty years after the tough-mother campaign began, it is still going strong—and they still set us apart from the crowd. You look at 90 percent of today's advertisements by manufacturers of outerwear or skiwear, and they are all the same: pictures of gorgeous people intertwined with each other who couldn't possibly do on skis what they're supposed to be doing. And then you've got me. The tall, thin, and blonde models in our competitors' ads may be easier on the eyes, but they don't care about you like good old Mother Boyle.

You can't really appreciate good advertisements without seeing them, so I invite you in the next pages to join me on a stroll down memory lane, as I share comments and memories of some of my favorite ads. And if you feel compelled by these ads to go out and buy a new Columbia jacket, then so much the better.

Here are a few of our print advertisements before we began the "tough mother" campaign in 1984. They may have made the point that our outerwear would keep people warm and dry, but they weren't very memorable and didn't separate us from our competitors.

ITEM: The Trinity Alps

TWO
ZIPPER-SECURED
POCKETS
(ONE INSIDE).

WIND FLAP
SECURES OVER
TWO-WAY
YKK COIL
ZIPPER.

STORM SKIRT
PREVENTS
HEAT LOSS.

FULLY-
ADJUSTABLE
GUSSETTED
VELCRO CUFFS.

For catalog, send $1 to:
Columbia Sportswear
6600 North Baltimore,
Portland, Oregon 97203
503/286-3676

Columbia
Sportswear Company
Portland, Oregon

DESCRIPTION:
Foul-weather Parka

SPECS:

Fabric: Gore-Tex laminated to
Taslan nylon. Inside: Gore-
Tex lets perspiration escape, but
blocks rain, mist, etc., completely. Outside: Durable, snag-
proof Taslan for long wear.
Insulation: Thinsulate. (150
gms/sq. meter.) Extends to full
length and hood.
Lining: Nylon taffeta.
Pockets: Total—6
Upper: 2 zipper-secured.
Lower: 2 Velcro-secured cargo
pockets with "bellows" pleats for
extra capacity. 2 additional
hidden hand-warming pockets
also lined with Thinsulate.
Hood: Permanent, full cut for
wear over headgear or alone.
Drawstring provides weather
seal and soft visor shields
glasses/goggles from rain.
Gen. Notes: Cut to size from
XXS-XL. Shell colors: Navy,
Green, Rust, Forest, Tan.
Trinity Alps: Parka No. 1642,
Made in Portland, Oregon.

We don't just design it. We engineer it.

ITEM: The Wallowa Vest

DESCRIPTION: Thermal Vest.

SNAG-WEAR
RESISTANT
POPLIN.

EXTRA TALL
INSULATED
COLLAR.

SPECS:

Fabric: Super tough Poplin
(65% polyester/35% cotton.)
Insulation: DuPont Dacron®
Hollofil™ II to provide
warmth even when wet.
(Washable.)
Pockets: Two two-way cargo/
handwarming pockets. Cargo
pocket seals with Velcro® for
secure storage. Handwarming
pockets fully insulated.
Zipper: Two-way #10 YKK
coil zipper.
Colors: Navy, Forest Green,
Tan, Rust, Silver.
The Wallowa Vest: No. 2152,
made in Portland, Oregon.
Sizes: XXS through XXXL.

INSULATED
ZIPPER
FLAP

ALL
EXTERIOR
SEAMS
TAPED.

REAR
KIDNEY
FLAP

For catalog, send $1 to:
Columbia Sportswear
6600 North Baltimore
Portland, Oregon 97203
503/286-3676

Columbia
Sportswear Company
Portland, Oregon

We don't just design it. We engineer it.

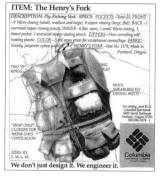

ITEM: The Henry's Fork

DESCRIPTION: Fly-Fishing Vest. SPECS: POCKETS –Total–33. FRONT
–9 Velcro closing (small, medium and large), 4 zipper closing (large, flat), BACK –1
oversized zipper closing pouch, INSIDE –6 flat, open, 1 small Velcro closing, 1
breast pocket, 1 oversized zipper-closing pouch. ZIPPERS – Non-corroding self-
healing plastic. COLOR – Dark moss green for exceptional camouflage. FABRIC –
Sturdy, polyester cotton poplin. HENRY'S FORK –Vest No. 1179; Made in
Portland, Oregon.

TWO "D"
RINGS

CLOSING
STRAP

WOOL
SHEARING FLY
DRYING PATCH

"SNAP ONLY"
CLOSURE FOR
WARM-DAYS
VENTILATION.

SIZES: XS,
S, M, L, XL.

For catalog, send $1 to
Columbia Sportswear
6600 North Baltimore
Portland, Oregon 97203
503/286-3676

Columbia
Sportswear Company
Portland, Oregon

We don't just design it. We engineer it.

"INTRODUCING THE PRODUCT OF AN OVERLY PROTECTIVE MOTHER."

—Tim Boyle

As a kid, when I wanted to go out and play, Mom would bundle me up like a knight about to plunge into battle.

Now, as President of Columbia, it appears she wants to do the same for you. Albeit a bit more efficiently.

Meet our new Palmer System IV Parka™ An outer jacket of Gore-Tex® over Exacta™ Cloth. And a zip-in *reversible* interior jacket of Polar Fleece on one side, Exacta™ Cloth on the other.

Figure it out. Worn together or separately, there are four jackets here, to cope with anything your adventures may lead to. Be it breeze, blizzard or black knight.

Finally a parka as changeable as the weather. The new Palmer™ is four jackets in one.

The Palmer System IV Parka™ is available at finer outfitters everywhere. For a color brochure send $1 to us at 6600 N. Baltimore, Dept. A1, Portland, Oregon 97203.
Gore-Tex® is a registered trademark of W.L. Gore & Assoc.
Za Pel® is a registered trademark of Dupont.

Columbia
Sportswear Company

"FROM ONE TOUGH MOTHER TO ANOTHER."
—Tim Boyle

To design, build and market a parka capable of withstanding the many temperaments of Mother Nature is no small task. But here's just the person for the job. My mother.

Her single-minded goal: to engineer the finest outerwear out there.

This Anacortes Parka is a prime example. There are literally hundreds of ways we could've made it cheaper. We could've used a shell of anything but Gore-Tex®, or not individually sealed each seam. We could've used less than 200 gram Thinsulate® insulation, left off the unique knit neckband, waist drawcord/snowbelt, and a few of the eight pockets. And who'd really notice if we hadn't taken the time to double-sew the seams and bartack all stress points?

You guessed it. Mother Boyle would.

And compared to her, Mother Nature is a pussycat.

Thinsulate

For color catalog, send $1 to us at 6600 N. Baltimore, Dept. O, Portland, Oregon 97203.
Gore-Tex® is a registered trademark of W.L. Gore & Assoc., Inc.
Thinsulate® is a registered trademark of 3M.

Columbia
Sportswear Company

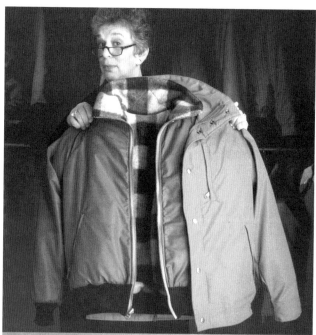

INTRODUCING THE INDUSTRY'S MOST VERSATILE SKI PARKA. (AND THE BULLHEADED MOTHER BEHIND IT.)

"When Mom took over running Columbia some years back, there were those who were skeptical. Nor any longer.

"We've grown over 600%. More importantly, she's constantly pushed for breakthrough ideas in outerwear engineering. While stubbornly adhering to some basic beliefs about work ethic, product quality and dealer responsiveness.

"You're looking at the latest evidence. The Palmer System IV Parka. We know of nothing else like it in the business.

Four Parkas in One.

"Inspired by our enormously successful Quad Parka for hunters, this version is tailored for skiers. The outer shell is Gore-Tex® laminated to Exacta™ Cloth, the zip-in interior is Polar Fleece and Exacta™ Cloth. And it's reversible.

"Either can be worn separately, both can be worn together. So whatever the weather dishes out, the Palmer can take.

Meet Both at Booth 1322.

"If you sense the exceptional sales potential of

this unique product, see it in person at SIA. As GM, I'll be there with the Palmer and several other intelligently engineered Columbia garments.

"And yes, Mother Gert Boyle will be there too. Just to keep all of us in line."—Tim Boyle

 Columbia
Sportswear Company

P.O. Box 03239, 6600 N. Baltimore, Portland, OR 97203
Toll-free call (800) 547-8066. In Oregon call 286-3676.

"'CAN'T WE BUILD A (☆!©#⚡) PARKA THAT DOESN'T IGNORE THE OBVIOUS,' STORMED MOTHER." —Tim Boyle

I'll be candid. Even though she's President of Columbia, my mother's not what you'd call an avid outdoorsman. Still, she recently observed something so painfully obvious that it should push parka technology ahead twenty years. It did for us.

Her revelation: Weather Changes.

While this may not sound overly profound to you, it is curious to us that apparently no jacket manufacturer has yet to notice this phenomenon. Including ourselves.

But we have just rectified the situation. Examine our Palmer System IV Parka.™ It is literally four jackets in one. The outer shell is of Gore-Tex® and Exacta™ Cloth. The zip-in *reversible* interior is buffalo plaid Polar Fleece on one side, Exacta™ Cloth on the other. The tall tunnel collar looks as good as it works.

Now, ponder the possibilities.

You're skiing early and it's colder than sin at the top of the lift. So you zip *both* shell and liner together for extraordinary warmth. Later, the sun comes out and you heat up. So you stow the liner and just go with the shell. For a little après activity you wear the rather dapper-looking buffalo plaid liner alone. Or reverse it for snugness.

Point being, here at long last is a parka as changeable as the weather.

Now, while other manufacturers may have failed to notice that the weather changes, we suspect they will be quick to notice that our parka does. So in a year or so you will probably be able to pick up a reasonably good copy of our Palmer.™

Or, you could go out and pick up an original now.

Something my mother would much more prefer.

Gore-Tex® is a trademark of W.L. Gore & Assoc., Inc.

Columbia
Sportswear Company

The Palmer System IV Parka™ is available at finer outfitters everywhere. For a color brochure send $1 to us at 6600 N. Baltimore, Dept. P1, Portland, Oregon 97203.

Sometimes the weather turns extremely cold.

Sometimes it turns cold and wet.

Sometimes it turns cold and crisp.

Sometimes it turns mild and wet or windy.

105

Our little company has grown pretty well over the years by engineering serious outerwear for serious outdoorsmen and women.

So when we decided to enter the skiwear market, our president (that's her to the right) handed down an edict. She's good at edicts.

I don't remember it word for word, but the gist of it was, Columbia is not going into the skiwear business with just another line of fancypants skiwear. We'd need something more technical, more advanced than anything out there.

Now, after considerable effort, we've done it.

"MY MOTHER REFUSES TO SELL A SINGLE PARKA TO SKIERS." —*Tim Boyle*

The Bugaboo! System™ of skiwear.

Far more than a collection of nicely coordinated garments, this is an entire new approach to wardrobing a skier. Through an ingenious zipper design, a number of parkas, jackets and vests can be worn by themselves or coupled together, as one. To cope with the wide swings in temperature from the lift lines to the lodge lounge.

There's a tough new outercloth called Bergundtal™ that repels moisture and wind alike. And a Jaeger Fleece™ that warms, insulates and resists pilling.

Certain models feature our patented new Radial Sleeve™ design that affords skiers a freedom of arm movement basically never before possible in a truly warm jacket.

Altogether there are five items in the system. For men and women. And, thanks to our exclusive Columbia Interchange System, the Bugaboo parka and vests can also be coupled with some eight other unique Columbia outerwear garments.

So if you're due for new skiwear this season, take a little motherly advice. Don't buy a single thing. Buy a system. Start looking for the Bugaboos!

Bugaboo Parka™ comes with rip-out Jaeger Fleece™ liner. Wear either piece alone or both together for extreme weather.

Gaitors and pants are of Bergundtal™ Cloth and both reversible for varied looks.

Jaeger Fleece
Bergundtal Cloth

Vest is reversible and can be worn solo or zipped into parka.

BUGABOO!

❖ Columbia Sportswear Company

For a color brochure send $1 to us at 4600 N. Baltimore, Dept. P3, Portland, Oregon 97203.

And, as usually happens when Mother thinks something's wrong, she does something about it. So, as Chairman of Columbia, she hereby introduces a whole new kind of apparel for athletes. (Well, the truth is Mother stole the idea. From our own Interchange skiwear system.)

Meet the Intertrainer.™ Actually three unique pieces of athletic wear in one.

"MOTHER THINKS IT'S RIDICULOUS THAT JOCKS DON'T HAVE ZIP-OUT FLEECE LINERS."

—Tim Boyle, President, Columbia Sportswear

First, a light, bright shell of nylon ripstop. Second, a multi-color jacket of our own ZAP fleece that wicks moisture away from the body. And third, the two of them zipped together to create a double layer of protection. Is this smart or what?

On mild days the shell is perfect. The fleece liner by itself makes sense for warming up or cooling down. And the two together work great for cooler temperatures and post-exercise warmth. Besides adapting to all kinds of weather conditions, it also adapts to all kinds of conditioning. So it's perfect for you crosstrainers.

Like all Columbia Sportswear items, the Intertrainer is thoughtfully constructed. With zip-pockets, elastic waist, collar tabs, and our patented Radial Sleeve for freer arm movement.

If the weather changes, so can your Intertrainer

If you're in the market for some legitimate athletic apparel, don't buy a single garment until you try on this three. Available for men and women. With pants and shorts to match.

Jocks never had it so comfy. Thanks to mom.

It's a shell.
It's a fleece jacket.
It's a combo of both.
Three degrees of protection in one.

Columbia
Sportswear Company
To find a Columbia dealer near you, call 1-800-MA BOYLE. In Canada, 1-299-9200. 5600 N. Baltimore St., Portland, Oregon 97203

"Protective, but not overly warm. Just like the parka."

—*Tim Boyle, President*

Mother Gert Boyle, Chairman

Although Mother is not terribly affectionate she does take a parental interest in everything we do, constantly hovering over our work. She calls it quality control. We call it unnerving. And unfortunately, the end usually justifies her means. Case in point, our Chukar™ Parka.

This upland garment is a breakthrough in lightweight (and light price) protection. The cotton duck cloth shell is breathable yet wind resistant. It's also warm, when worn with the amazing Zap™-Fleece liner, a Columbia exclusive. Zap-Fleece wicks away perspiration, warding off chill in cold weather yet ventilating in warm.

Additional features of the Chukar include Radial™ Sleeves for uninhibited movement, shooting patch, rear game pouch and our Columbia Interchange System™ for wearing shell or liner solo. All very thoughtful touches, mandated by you-know-who. In spite of her outward appearance, she still has a mother's instinct.

Columbia
Sportswear Company

6600 N. Baltimore, Portland, OR 97223
For the Columbia dealer nearest you, call 1-800-MA-BOYLE
In Canada, 1-503-291-8200

Gert Boyle, Chairman, Columbia Sportswear

QUOTES FROM CHAIRMAN MA.

INSPIRATION FROM MOTHER BOYLE, THE SKIWEAR
REVOLUTIONARY WHO KOWTOWS TO NO ONE.

"Follow the correct path to outdoor comfort, through the Columbia Interchange System."

"All that is required to overcome adversity are reinforced stress points, double sewn seams, taller tunnel collars, and storm flaps."

"Am I the only one who thinks in this business?"

"Evolution through adaptation: when the weather changes, one's ski parka had better change with it."

"A sensible and functional design is well-suited to the masses. Have it on my desk tomorrow."

"I asked for a fifth outside pocket. Not how much it would cost."

"A reversible liner that is also weatherproof? Sounds impossible. Build me one."

"It's perfect. Now make it better."

The 4-in-1 Gizzmo® Parka: Bergundtal Cloth™ outershell, reversible Thinsulate® liner with Hydro Plus™ weatherproofing. Wear either separately, or zip together for maximum protection.

❖ Columbia
Sportswear Company

6600 N. Baltimore, Portland OR 97203. For the dealer nearest you call 1-800-MA-BOYLE. In Canada, 1-503-295-8081

110

ALL THE RAGE.

OUR CHAIRMAN PROVIDES ALL THE MOTIVATION WE NEED
TO STAY ON TOP OF THE SKIWEAR HEAP. *By Tim Boyle.*

If not for Mother's tempestuous nature, I doubt our skiwear would be the most popular in America. The woman is absolutely passionate about craftsmanship, and unrelenting in its application.

Consider our Bugaboo Parka™ The Bergundtal Cloth™ shell and removable Alpen Fleece™ liner combine via the Columbia Interchange System™ to form a third garment, while a storm flap and tunnel collar lend added protection. For mobility, both layers incorporate our diamond-shaped

Radial Sleeve™ underarm. For convenience, the roomy security pockets are accessible even when wearing thick gloves.

These standard features make the Bugaboo a model of sensible design, down to every reinforced stress point. No single detail has been overlooked. If by chance one was, we would've heard about it by now. As would have the folks in the next county.

◆ Columbia
Sportswear Company

6600 N. Baltimore, Portland OR 97203. For the dealer nearest you call 1-800-MA-BOYLE. In Canada, 1-503-295-8000.

Fall 1991: The truth is . . . I wouldn't hurt a fly. We even printed some greeting cards with this photograph on the front. The inscription inside the card? "Write me or ELSE!"

111

WRITE ME
or Else!

Columbia Sportswear Company is
proud to announce the birth of its
Flagship Retail Store

SORRY
I ALMOST
forgot YOUR
BIRTHDAY

GREETINGS
from the gang

"I KNOW WHAT *men* LIKE"

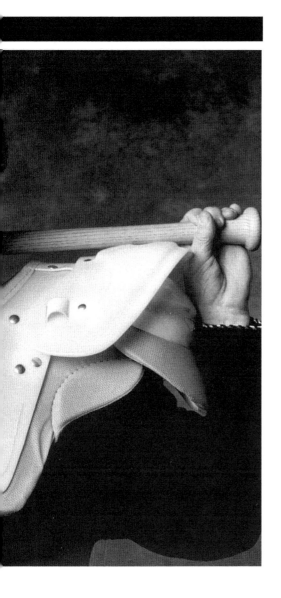

Fall 1992: A photograph of me next to the word "Sexy." P. T. Barnum was wrong.

*Mother Ge
Chairman, Columbia Sp*

"IN OREGON THIS IS SEXY."

–By Tim Boyle, President, Columbia Sportswear

Up here in the Northwest ...ke a rather ...al view of ...is appeal-... Mother ...t, then it ...olumbia ...wear's ulti-...uthority ...she insists ...auty must ...ake the place ...ctionality. ...aybe that attitude ...s from working in Portland, ...on. Where variety in the daily weather pat-...onsists of rain-sun, rain-sun, sun-rain. ...elieve me, when the weather turns nasty, ...ng is more attractive than a parka that ...adapts to the elements.

...at's where the Gizzmo Parka™ comes ...terms of practicality, it speaks for itself.

But I'll throw in my two cents anyway.

The Gizzmo starts with a weatherproof Bergundtal Cloth™ outer-shell. Inside, we insert a reversible Ther-moloft® liner, which itself has a waterproof Hydro Plus™ shell. You take it from there. Wear the outershell separately if it's rainy, but warm. On a chilly night, you may opt to wear the liner alone. Or reverse the liner to change colors. Or, if Mother Nature's dander is really up, zip the shell and liner together for maximum protection. All in all, the Gizzmo is four parkas in one.

Sometimes determining what is sexy is merely a matter of how efficiently you can cover things up.

Columbia
Sportswear Company

Baltimore, Portland, Oregon 97203. For the dealer nearest you in the U.S. and Canada call 1-800-MA-BOYLE.

119

Mother Gert I
Chairman, Columbia Sports

"SHE SNAPS NECKS AND HACKS OFF ARMS."

–By Tim Boyle, President, Columbia Sportswear

My Mother, Columbia Sportswear's chairman, will stop at nothing to get what she wants–superior outerwear.

In fact, the mountains around Portland, Oregon, frequently echo her sharply barked commands. "When I say a snap closed neck and storm front, that's what I expect to see!" Or, as she hacks away at an inappropriately attached sleeve, "All seams are to be double sewn!"

What, you may ask, is the end result of having such a, uh, vociferous chairman? The Columbia Interchange System, for one. It lets you brave multiple weather conditions with one jacket by matching a zip-in, zip-out liner to a weatherproof shell. They may be worn separately, or together. Take our Ponderosa Parka™ pictured here. The outer shell is 100% Technicloth II™–a soft blend of cotton and nylon woven into a durable rib fabric, oiled to keep water out. To hold warmth in, the bomber-style Zap Fleece™ liner is quilted with Thermoloft™ insulation.

All in all, it's easy to see why not just any parka can survive Mother's rather pointed demands.

Columbia
Sportswear Company

121

Fall 1993: I don't know why it took so long for them to come up with this one. How do you get a then sixty-nine-year-old woman across some very slippery rocks to pose under a waterfall? Very carefully.

Mother
Chairman, Columbia

Fall 1993: The ultimate bad hair day. It took some convincing to get me to pose for this one. After all, I spent hours every morning to look halfway decent, and then they ruined it all in five minutes.

Mother Gert Boyle
Chairman, Columbia Sportswear

"A RADICAL CONCEPT FROM MOTHER BOYLE."

–By Tim Boyle, President, Columbia Sportswear

If you ever met my mother, you know that a fiercely independent Oregonian. ...sions... e is man, ...mbia ...swear blaze the trails of America's outerwear industry.

Take the Gizzmo Parka™ as an example of fearlessness in the face of convention. Who else could so skillfully blend colors like blueberry and ultraviolet in a jacket? And who else has my mother's futuristic vision when it comes to flexibility? After all, she pioneered the Interchange System,™ embodied here in the Gizzmo Parka. It's one of a long line of all-weather Columbia parkas that feature the zip-in, zip-out liner, creating three-parkas-in-one.

As president, I'm the first one to applaud my mother's regular departures from the norm. But I think those earrings are a bit much.

Gizzmo Parka™

Columbia
Sportswear Company

Baltimore, Portland, Oregon 97203. For the dealer nearest you in the U.S. and Canada call 1-800-MA BOYLE.

You can't believe how many people saw this ad, assumed the tattoo was real, and asked me to show it to them. I'll let you in on a little secret—the "tattoo" washed off. I understand, however, that "Born to Nag" is now featured in catalogs on tattoo parlors. If there's a woman out there who actually had "Born to Nag" tattooed on her arm, please let me know—I'll send you a Columbia jacket!

128

"MOTHER CREATED THE BUGABOO BECAUSE GOD CREATED THE BUGABOOS."

—Tim Boyle, President, Columbia Sportswear

Mother Boyle, Chairman

Somewhere in British Columbia, Mother Nature unzips an enormous black cloud, dumping an icy torrent on the Bugaboo Mountains. Then the sun shines. Then it doesn't. All in a span of, oh, say twenty minutes. Somewhere in Portland, Oregon, Mother Boyle zips a nonpilling, MTR fleece liner into a weatherproof shell. Whoever wears this three-in-one parka is ready to meet the schizophrenic weather on the Bugaboos face-to-face. Matter of fact, they're ready to face just about any weather, anywhere.

Bugaboo Parka,™ Portland, Oregon

Columbia
SportswearCompany

6600 N. Baltimore, Portland, Oregon 97203. For the dealer nearest you in the U.S. and Canada call 1-800-MA BOYLE.

129

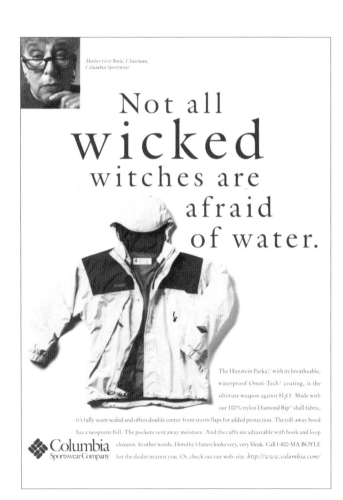

Mother Gert Boyle, Chairman, Columbia Sportswear

Not all
wicked
witches are
afraid
of water.

The Hunstein Parka™ with its breatheable, waterproof Omni-Tech™ coating, is the ultimate weapon against H_2O. Made with our 100% nylon Diamond Rip™ shell fabric, it's fully seam sealed and offers double center-front storm flaps for added protection. The roll-away hood has a neoprene bill. The pockets vent away moisture. And the cuffs are adjustable with hook and loop closures. In other words, Dorothy's future looks very, very bleak. Call 1-800-MA BOYLE for the dealer nearest you. Or, check out our web-site. *http://www.columbia.com/*

Columbia
Sportswear Company

SHE'D MOVE TO FLORIDA
BUT THE WEATHER SUCKS THERE.

Retiring to the beach to play a little shuffleboard? Not in this lifetime. Chairman Mother Gert Boyle's too busy making the Fire Ridge Parka. Its Columbia Interchange System with 100% nylon Bergundtal Cloth, pull-out hood and heathered MTR Fleece zip-out liner make sure it won't be confused for a bikini. After all, Florida's a nice place to visit, but you wouldn't want to live there. For a dealer near you call 1-800-MA BOYLE.

www.columbia.com

131

OVERBEARING TYRANT.

IT HAS A NICE RING TO IT.

Sure you appreciate company Chairman Gert Boyle's fanatical attention to detail. You don't have to work with her. You don't have to stay up until the wee hours sweating the details. You just  get to wear the

stuff. Like the Tumbleweed Pullover™. With heavy duty Rock Pile™, Radial Sleeves™, comfy pockets and antiqued brass zippers, it's got late-night lattes written all over it. But then again, things aren't always so tough working with Gert. After we finish a jacket we can just think back to her tender words, "A team effort is everyone doing what I say." Kinda makes you feel all warm inside.

Columbia Sportswear Company®

For the dealer nearest you call 1-800-MA KWELL. www.columbia.com

STAY AS
WARM
AND DRY
AS HER
POT ROAST.

The one time you'll enjoy being treated like a piece of meat. Because that's the purpose of Columbia's Spitfire Parka™. To make sure you end up like one of Chairman Gert Boyle's pot roasts: comfortably warm and dry as a bone. But on you, these conditions result from the use of superior materials rather than overcooking. A lining of nylon tafetta quilted to Slimtech™ keeps the warm in, while a Bergundtal Cloth™ outer shell keeps the wet out. And fortunately, warm and dry is more appetizing on you than on a three pound slab of beef.

Columbia
Sportswear Company®

For the dealer nearest you call 1-800-MA BOYLE. www.columbia.com

WHEN YOU ARE AS OLD AS THE HILLS,

YOU TEND TO KNOW WHAT TO WEAR IN THEM.

Chairman Gert Boyle's 75 years of life experience go into every garment she designs. Columbia's Dolomite Parka™ is no exception. A Bergundtal Cloth™ shell makes it tough enough to ward off any

weather condition, but the Bergundtal Ripstop™ reinforcements make it that much more tough. And the zip-out Perfecta Cloth™ and MTR Fleece™ liner keeps you comfortably warm well down into painfully cold,

Columbia
Sportswear Company®

single-digit temperatures. So for your next trek into the cold,

take it from the voice of wisdom: Wear a Dolomite Parka.

For the dealer nearest you call 1-800-MA BOYLE. www.columbia.com

137

FRIGID PERHAPS.

COLD NEVER.

has my face on it? "I earned every one of those wrinkles."

Throughout her life, Chairman Gert Boyle has been called many things. Cold, however, has never been one of them. Probably something to do with the Boulder Ridge Parka™ that she is never without. She designed it herself using the Columbia Interchange System,™ with a Bergundtal Cloth™ shell and Bergundtal Ripstop II™ reinforcements on the outside, zip-out Perfecta Cloth™ and MTR Fleece™ lining on the inside. Because if there's one thing she's learned in 74 years, it's how to stay warm. For the dealer nearest you call 1-800-MA BOYLE, www.columbia.com

Columbia
Sportswear Company.

SHE'D
GLADLY RETIRE
WHEN HELL
FREEZES OVER,
BUT THAT'S
WHEN
WE'LL NEED
HER MOST.

When it comes to Chairman Gert Boyle, you're best off just getting used to her.
cause she plans on ruling until the bitterly cold end with her winter arsenal at
side. An arsenal that includes the Bugabootoo. The boot with waterproof,
l-grain leather upper, double latex seam-sealed construction, and 200g
ermolite insulation. And more important to you, the boot that'll make
e you come out on top in the age-old battle of foot vs. nature. For the
er nearest you call 1-800-MA BOYLE. www.columbia.com

Columbia
Sportswear Company.

UNOS DÍAS
A SOLAS
CON ELLA Y
TERMINARÁS
POR
ENCONTRARLA
ENCANTADORA

A primera vista, el encanto de una mujer de 75 años puede pasar desapercibido. Pero seguro que empiezas a mirarla con otros ojos si piensas que Ma' Boyle Boyle, P.–D.G. de Columbia Sportswear, ha sido quien ha concebido las Bugabootoo. Las botas que mantendrán tus pies calientes y secos cuando el suelo esté frío y embarrado. El empeine en piel flor impermeable, el casco moldeado por inyección, las costuras de doble hilo hidrófobo selladas con látex y 900 gramos de aislamiento Thermolite son suficientes razones para que cambies tu punto de vista. Especialmente a 35° bajo cero. Además, son ligeras como una pluma para que llevarlas no te cueste sudores. **Columbia** Sportswear Company

Los productos Columbia Sportswear se encuentran en las mejores tiendas especializadas de Oregón y del resto del mundo. También puede encontrar Columbia Sportswear en Internet: http://www.columbia.com

143

RUMORS PERSIST THAT GRANDMOTHERS ARE KIND AND GENTLE.

We've heard the rumors too. It's just that working around Columbia Chairman Gert Boyle and her hard-nosed way of getting things done, you tend to forget them. Fortunately, this unrelenting determination does have some benefits. Like the comfort of the Pinedale Oxford™. A four-layer cushioning system combines with a wicking lining to keep things dry and comfortable, while a full-grain leather upper and multi-directional outsole provides support and traction. It makes it the perfect shoe for home, office and any point in between. For a dealer near you call 1-800-MA BOYLE.

Columbia
Sportswear Company®
www.columbia.com

THEY SAY ICE PUMPS THROUGH HER VEINS.
THAT'S ASSUMING SHE HAS A HEART.

Heart or no heart, Columbia Chairman Gert Boyle has devoted a lifetime to defeating the cold. The Fire Ridge Parka™ is testament to that. Its Bergundtal Cloth™ shell keeps the cold away while an MTR Fleece™ liner and pull-out hood keep the warm comfortably where it belongs. Because when it comes right down to it, who cares if she has a heart so long as ice isn't pumping through your veins. For a dealer near you call 1-800-MA BOYLE.

Columbia
Sportswear Company®
www.columbia.com

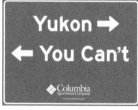

Chairman Gert Boyle

IT'S OFTEN SAID THAT
PEOPLE RESEMBLE THEIR PETS.

Let's compare. On the right, the Johnny Rail™ shoe. A thing of beauty complete with a craggy multi-directional lug sole for outstanding grip, a rough leather and mesh upper for toughness and breathability and a gnarly toe-cap overlay for serious off-road duty. On the left, company chairman and dour princess of product quality, Gert Boyle. Yes, that sure is one nice looking shoe. For a dealer nearest you call 1-800-MA BOYLE.

Columbia
Sportswear Company.

www.columbia.com

147

Fall 2003: Believe it or not, I received more mail about this ad than any other in Columbia's history. Who knew that the "s word" would unleash such a firestorm?

TITANIUM

colu

WHEREVER SNOT FREEZES, WE'LL BE THERE.

Fall 1990: In our first television commercial, I put Tim and our Columbia Interchange System through a car wash. Tim was an incredibly good—and soggy—sport throughout the filming. We arrived early in the morning, and did take after take for literally the entire day. In order to star in Columbia's commercials, both of us had to become members of the Screen Actors Guild. If any movie producers are interested in a remake of *Pretty Woman,* I'm available.

Fall 1994: Tim and I demonstrate the strength of our Columbia Parka in what was my favorite commercial. We actually had stunt doubles during the filming process. They even made a mask of my face and put it on my double: the poor woman probably still hasn't recovered. It took four men to lift me to a rock during the taping. I told them that if anyone grunted, they were fired.

151

Fall 1997: To test our latest parka, I strap Tim to the roof of my car and head for the mountains. We filmed this in Banff, Alberta, and Tim and I had stunt doubles again. During the filming, the stunt driver went too fast, and ran a brand-new car with only twelve miles on it into a ditch. The stuntman strapped to the roof, who was also a professional bull rider, commented later that he had never been so scared in his life.

  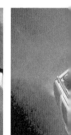

Fall 2001: I throw Tim to the sled dogs to test the warmth and durability of Columbia's outerwear. I actually got to ride a dogsled when we filmed this commercial in Central Oregon. The magic of Hollywood—after two days of filming outside in the snow, the director decided he didn't like the backdrop, so we moved to a warm studio and filmed against a "blue screen."

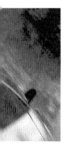

TESTED TOUGH

Fall 2001: I was seventy-seven years old when I got to drive my first Zamboni. In this commercial, I run the Zamboni over Tim who was encased in Plexiglas. It was just like driving a riding lawnmower. The funny thing is that even though Tim has been in a number of our television and print ads, nobody ever recognizes him. That's proof that all eyes are on the old lady.

TESTED TOUGH

Arnold and I have much in common—both immigrants who went on to become sex symbols.

7

I MEET THE MOST INTERESTING PEOPLE

In 1989, I turned sixty-five years old. And while I certainly wasn't ready to retire, it seemed time to officially recognize the fact that Tim deserved the title of President and CEO, and I began my service as Chairman. (I never did like the word "Chairwoman," and I couldn't convince Tim that we should be the first company to have an official "ChairMa.") Tim has run the day-to-day operations of the company ever since, and I have focused my efforts on serving as the public face of Columbia Sportswear. And what a face it is!

On most days, I wake up about 6:30 A.M. and am out the door by 8:00, usually joined by a bagel with cream cheese and a cup of coffee. I arrive at the office about thirty minutes later, ready to put in a full day. I normally leave around 4:00 P.M. or so and usually exercise with friends three nights a week. Just in case we might have lost a pound or two, we then go out to dinner.

If I'm not in the office, then I'm likely to be on the road, promoting Columbia Sportswear. Tim and I still believe in listening to our customers, and there aren't many major sportswear and outerwear industry conventions or shows where one or both of us are not in attendance. While at these gatherings, I just plop myself down in front of the Columbia booth and talk to anyone who passes by. I still occasionally receive double takes from people who had always assumed that I was an actress hired to portray a role in our advertisements, and can't believe that there is actually a real Ma Boyle. Hard to think they thought that someone could make a living in Hollywood with a face like mine!

Many of my friends urge me to take it easier, and to spend more time taking it easy. That's just the not the way I am wired. Besides, I think that my coming to work every day sends a statement that folks in their so-called golden years can still make a meaningful contribution in the workplace. I have always believed that experience is an asset, and that older workers are of great value to a business. Perhaps my presence in the office offers a message that managers who like to put older workers out to pasture are out to lunch.

Not only are older workers good for a business, but business is also good for older workers. One of my secrets to staying young is that I have the opportunity to work with young people. When I travel to foreign countries on Columbia's behalf, I'm usually joined by a handful of folks from our sales or public relations staff, most of whom are less than half my age. (Hell, some of our new employees who are just out of college are barely a quarter of my age!) I take great pride, however, in keeping a full schedule during these trips, while many of them are still in the hotel room suffering from jet lag. My tip for surviving business travel is to sit down on the plane, go to sleep, and then wake up a few hours later. I also don't take along a computer or a cell phone. I focus on what's ahead of me—not what I left behind in the office.

One of the fun and surprising parts of my life has been the opportunity to cross paths with a number of prominent leaders and celebrities who I never imagined I would meet. Some of these meetings were especially memorable as I stuck my foot (clad, of course, in Columbia Sportswear shoes) in my mouth.

For instance, I was at an awards dinner in New York City when I introduced myself to a pleasant looking woman who said her name was "Mary Kay." "What do you do?" I asked her. She responded, "Well, I own a cosmetic company." "Oh, you're *that* Mary Kay," I said. "If you had been in your pink Cadillac I would have known who you were."

I did something similar a while later in New Mexico, where Columbia was sponsoring the annual Albuquerque

Hot Air Balloon Festival. I had spent nearly half an hour having a delightful conversation with a gentleman named Gary when I finally asked him what he did. "I'm the governor," he said. "Of this state?" I asked. "You got it," Governor Gary Johnson replied. And I said, "What the hell is a nice guy like you doing in politics?"

Then there was the time our public relations people came to me and said that singer Jimmy Buffet was going to be performing in Portland, and that he was a fan of Columbia apparel and wanted the opportunity to meet me. On the night of the concert, I was ushered backstage and told that Jimmy would be there soon. The only problem was that while I had heard his songs, I had no idea what he looked like. My daughter Kathy joined me at the concert and was mortified when I pointed to every man that walked by—be they young or old, black or white—and asked if they were Jimmy. I should add that once we did meet, Jimmy was very charming and gracious, and we agreed that everyone in Margaritaville should wear a Columbia jacket.

Another true gentleman is comedian Jerry Seinfeld, whom I had the opportunity to meet when he came to Portland in January 2004. Our flagship store was just a block away from the hotel where Seinfeld was staying, and he paid a visit to lend some publicity for CASA, an organization I have long supported that helps abused and neglected children. I insisted that Jerry choose a jacket as a gift from me, and personally helped to fit him. When the local newspaper later asked me what I thought of Jerry, I said that I couldn't help but notice that he had a good body. I was very impressed that Jerry took time to greet employees and customers, and to sign a jacket, which was later auctioned off by CASA for several thousand dollars.

Some of the most rewarding experiences of my life have come through my involvement with Special Olympics. My interest in this program began when the United States Special Olympics team asked Columbia to assist in outfitting them for their World Games. The more I learned about this inspiring organization, the more I knew that Columbia should play a small part in its success.

I then had the opportunity to meet Eunice Shriver, the founder of Special Olympics. What a remarkable woman! Eunice and her son, Tim, speak with such passion about the difference that Special Olympics makes in the life of young Americans with disabilities. I saw that difference firsthand when I met with a number of amazing Special Olympic athletes, and was able to witness how they courageously persevere through tremendous challenges.

At Eunice's invitation, I later attended Special Olympic competitions and events in Canada, Alaska, Ireland, and South Africa. While at these events, I became friends with Eunice's daughter, Maria, and her husband, then-actor and now California Governor, Arnold Schwarzenegger. Maria is a delight. She has an ability to form an almost instant rapport with literally every Special Olympic athlete. I can also report that the tough mother and the Terminator hit it off right away. I found Arnold to be a very intelligent individual with a wonderful sense of humor.

I was once seated next to Arnold at a Special Olympic fund-raising auction, where one of the items up for bids was a *Terminator* script that he had signed. Also at our table was a wealthy businessman whom I found to be a little bit of a blowhard. I'm sure he had a rather dim view of me, as when he asked me what I did, I told him that I was a seamstress. When he announced that he wanted that script, I couldn't help myself and began to bid against him. I don't recall what that script ended up costing me, but since all the money went to Special Olympics, it was worth every penny.

My journey to South Africa on behalf of Special Olympics was very memorable, as I had the opportunity to meet former South African President Nelson Mandela. The group meeting with Mandela included Eunice and Tim Shriver, Arnold Schwarzenegger, me, and a delegation of Special Olympic athletes. The meeting was made even more unforgettable by the fact that it was held on Robben Island, home to the prison where Mandela was locked up for twenty-five years by the South African government. Our delegation traveled by boat to the island, which is seven miles off the coast of Capetown. We then walked five hundred yards or so to the gates of the prison, where Mandela was awaiting us. Upon seeing Arnold, he dropped into a boxer's crouch, pretending he was ready to go a few rounds with the movie star. He then went over to the young athletes, taking time to smile and talk with each one of them. The Shrivers and a few other Special Olympic leaders then escorted Mandela into a small meeting room for a conversation on how the program could be expanded in South Africa. A few minutes went by, and Tim Shriver came out of the meeting, yelled my name, and motioned me into the room. I've never been accused of being the silent type, but I was so awed by Mandela that I simply couldn't bring myself to say very much during our meeting with him. I was able, however, to present him with a Columbia Sportswear jacket, and watching him put it on almost moved this tough mother to tears.

I didn't think that thrill could be topped, but the Special Olympics moment that remains the most moving and memorable was the time when the mother of one of the athletes told me that her son's most treasured possession was his uniform bearing the Columbia Sportswear logo. "This is the first uniform he ever had," she explained. "It's the first time someone has honored him for who he is."

While Columbia's success has changed my bank account, and has allowed me to support a variety of philanthropies, it hasn't changed who I am. That comes as a surprise to some people. I have lost count of the number of times someone comes up to me in a grocery store and asks what I'm doing shopping in a grocery store, evidently assuming that I would have someone do that for me. I respond by saying, "I'm shopping because I like to eat." I tried hiring a secretary on a couple of occasions, but it never worked out. I like doing my own stuff. I like answering my phone. I like reading and answering my mail. I hate housework, so I do have a butler named Charlie. The problem is that he's a 5'7" wooden statue I bought in Hawaii. The bad news is he doesn't do floors or windows. The good news is that he doesn't talk back.

A cup of coffee . . . a piece of my apple pie . . . and some advice from Mother Boyle. . . . Is there a better way to start the day?

8

MA BOYLE'S RECIPES

There was a Greek poet named Sophocles who once wrote, "One must wait until the evening to see how splendid the day has been." At eighty years of age, I suppose that I am in the evening—*early* evening—of my life. And as I look back on it, I can say that the day has been truly splendid: wonderful parents, a country that took a family of immigrants in and allowed us to prosper, a husband who was my best friend every day of our twenty-two years of marriage, three children who have all succeeded, five grandchildren who help keep me young, interesting friends, the ability to contribute to organizations that make a positive difference in the lives of others, and the opportunity to show up each day at a job I love and work with intelligent and creative people. Who could ask for more?

When people ask me what my plans are for the years ahead, I often answer by telling them I want to be thin, blonde, and sexy. Don't hold your breath. What I do look forward to is coming to work and doing what I can to help Columbia remain at the top of our field in terms of quality and creativity. And when my time comes, I might just keep coming to work. Tim has long said that when I go, he's going to have me stuffed and permanently placed in the entryway of our headquarters. That suits me just fine—as long as I'm dressed head to toe in Columbia products.

The question I am probably asked more often than any other is "How did Columbia do it?" In other words, why did Columbia survive and succeed beyond my wildest expectations when other companies in the industry—with more money, a larger national presence, and more experienced leaders—sputtered or went bankrupt? The fact of the matter is there is no easy answer to that question, but what follows are what I believe were the steps and decisions most responsible for Columbia's success.

Ma Boyle's Recipe for Success in Business

1. Don't give up. Winston Churchill had it about right when he said, "Never give in, never give in, never, never, never, never—in nothing, great or small, large or petty, never give in except to convictions of honor and good sense." The only way I would improve upon Churchill's advice is to add a few more nevers. There were countless times in the years following Neal's death when Tim and I were told that we needed to sell Columbia. Thank heavens that the one time we listened to their advice, the man buying the company turned out to be such a jerk that I eventually told him where he could go. Every business has its ups and downs, and if you are tempted to give up when times are tough, then just think of how different my life would have turned out if the sale had gone through. Let's face it. I was a housewife and a mother, and Tim

was a twenty-one-year-old college student when fate put us at the helm of Columbia. While we may not have had business experience, we did have tenacity. It was that tenacity that allowed Columbia to survive, while giving us time to get the necessary experience.

2. Just because you can't give up doesn't mean you can't make a strategic retreat. There's a difference between throwing in the towel and turning the towel into a washcloth. There was a time when Columbia had to become smaller in order to continue, reducing the number of our employees and the number of our products. It was a painful process but maintaining the status quo was not an option, as the company would not have survived. There's nothing wrong with taking a little time to lick your wounds, as long as you remain focused on coming back stronger than ever.

3. Self-examination is better than self-defense. The biggest mistake that Tim and I made during our first rocky year in charge was to forget this motto, which had been a favorite of my late husband's. It's easy,

especially when times are tough, to adopt an "us versus them" mentality, and to think that anyone who questions your decisions is questioning your competence. Columbia began moving in the right direction when Tim and I started listening to the wisdom and experience of people who knew more than we did. We still do.

4. Listen to your customers and give them what they want. I know this is pure common sense, but you would be surprised at how many businesses just don't get it. There might not be a Columbia Sportswear if Neal hadn't listened to our customers who demanded a better fishing vest. It was also the reaction of our customers that moved Tim and me to approve the Ma Boyle ad campaign. I can't imagine a new Columbia product entering the marketplace without our designers seeking the input of our customers throughout the development process—a process that leads to a good product at a fair price.

5. Business is just another word for team. Because we are the public face of Columbia, Tim and I get a lot of credit for its success. It's true that we couldn't have done it without each other, but it's also true that we couldn't have done it without the help of hundreds upon hundreds of men and women who have been part of the Columbia team. There is only one way to treat a member of your team, and that's with respect. One of the most important parts of my job is roaming through the halls of our headquarters and talking with the members of our team, and I don't just talk work. I also ask them about their families and their life outside the office. I don't just worry about keeping our customers warm and dry; I also worry about keeping the members of our team challenged and rewarded.

6. Focus on what makes you unique. One of the best pieces of advice Tim and I received from our informal board of advisors was that Columbia made too many products that our competitors made just as well, and

that we should focus on the ones that were unique to us. Years later, our advertising agency sold us on a new campaign that would highlight the fact that having a mother and son running the company was unique in our industry. Even if you don't have an eighty-year-old grandmother as your chairman, there is still something that sets your business apart from your competitors—make the most of that difference.

7. Don't spend money you don't have, and be careful in spending the money you do. When Tim and I took the helm of Columbia we pinched every penny because every penny was needed. And while the business makes a lot more pennies these days, we are still pretty careful in spending them. Once a week or so you can find me behind my desk signing a pile of employee expense checks. There's a reason why I do this, and it's not that I don't trust the members of our team to file honest reports. I do trust them, and they know that. They also know that since I will be reviewing their hotel and restaurant bills they have

to be able to justify how they were spending the company's money. Tim and I could also give you quite a lengthy list of outerwear and sporting goods companies that have gone bankrupt these past few decades, many due to the fact that they borrowed more money then they could pay back.

8. Walk before you run. I saw many businesses in our industry make a quick splash and then go belly-up because they tried to do too much too fast. Columbia has experienced remarkable growth since Tim and I showed up that first day in December 1970, but we never grew beyond what we could afford, and we never allowed growth to diminish the quality of our products.

9. Always tell the truth, and you won't have to bother remembering the lies you told. My photograph is usually featured next to a witty or funny Columbia slogan in one of our advertisements. I am very proud of these ads, which have been instrumental to our success. I am also proud of a sign in the employee cafeteria at our company headquarters that includes

a picture of me and these very serious words: "Our success depends on our character, integrity, and trustworthiness." This statement may not be very catchy, but it's absolutely true. There is simply no substitute for honesty. You can't help but look at some of the corporate scandals of these past years and conclude that some people are so crooked that when they die, they will have to be screwed into the ground. All of these scandals can be traced back to someone not telling the truth. Tim and I have always prided ourselves on being honest with each other, honest with our investors, honest with our employees, and honest with our customers. Besides telling people who have never met me that I'm really thin, tall, and blonde, I can't recall ever lying in the course of business.

10. Do your best every day, and if you don't do your best one day, then do better tomorrow. I have tried to keep this simple thought in mind from that first day in December 1970 when I walked into Columbia's headquarters as the boss, rather than the boss's wife.

It was often tough—especially in the early years—to focus on the task at hand, especially when I was also trying to be a good mother, a good daughter, and a good friend. But if you just get up each morning with the attitude that you will do your best, and if you can't, then you will do better tomorrow, then no challenge seems insurmountable.

Ma Boyle's Recipe for Success in Life:

It's great to have succeeded in business, but I know I would be the same person had Columbia not done so well. Far more important than achieving success as great businessmen or women, is achieving success as a great *person*. Forgive my motherly instincts, as I offer advice on how to do just that:

1. Don't give up. See Rule Number 1 for Success in Business. The same applies for success in life. Don't give up. Yes there will be times when life knocks you down; when you lose a loved one, when you don't get that job you wanted. No one gets through life without

suffering some setbacks. The test is how you react to those setbacks. Do you retreat into a shell and live life in the past? Or do you draw strength from tough times, and look ahead to the future?

2. Keep family first. Every family is dysfunctional, and some are a little more dysfunctional than others, but placing your family as your top priority remains key to success in life. Most parents don't have the opportunity to work with their kids, and I wouldn't recommend it for every family. What I would suggest, however, is making sure that work leaves you plenty of time to spend with your spouse, your children, and your grandchildren.

3. Remember that whatever you think you are, someone else has probably been for a long time. My father's motto is just as wise today as it was when I first heard it many years ago. Simply put, don't take yourself too seriously.

4. Laugh. It's that simple. Not a day goes by when I'm not laughing with friends, family, and coworkers, or

laughing at myself. Even when the future didn't look too bright for Columbia, I was always able to laugh.

5. Volunteer: No matter what you do, and no matter your age, but most especially if you are in your "golden years"—find a mission or an organization that inspires you. For me, it has been Special Olympics and CASA. There are hundreds of worthy causes in every community. Getting out and making a difference is better than staying in and making yourself lonely.

6. Money doesn't make you any nicer or any smarter. There are some folks out there who now hang on my every word but who didn't give me the time of day when Columbia was struggling. I am still the same person now that I was back then. And I suppose they are the same person, too—someone who is a little bit on the phony side. Just because someone may have a big bank account doesn't mean that they become a better person. It's the size of your character and your heart that matter—not the size of your wallet.

7. Send thank-you notes. Call me old-fashioned if you like, but I still think that if someone gives you a gift or brightens your day, then a thank-you note is in order, and it will tell others quite a bit about the type of person you are. I'm talking about one that you write, put in an envelope, and send through the mail—e-mailing a thank-you note on the computer doesn't count.

8. Grandchildren are for spoiling. If you're lucky enough to have grandchildren, then there's nothing wrong with spoiling them on occasion. But if they violate rule Number 7 and don't send a thank-you note after you give them a gift, then don't give them another one until they see the error of their ways.

9. Don't let anyone—including yourself—put you in a box. Some of my friends in high school had life all mapped out—what they would wear the next day, the college they would attend, what sorority or fraternity they would pledge, and so on. The problem was they weren't leaving any room for that thing called life.

There's nothing wrong with planning—but I never planned on moving to America, and I never planned on becoming CEO and chair of one of America's largest sporting goods companies. Like a roller coaster, life has its ups and downs and twists and turns. Enjoy the ride.

10. You are never too old to learn. The overwhelming majority of people at my age are retired. I don't know how they do it; I can't imagine not coming to work. I know that not every senior citizen can or wants to work, but every senior citizen should keep working his or her mind. Find a subject you know nothing about and learn all you can. When you're done with that subject, pick another one. If you're physically able, take an exercise class. Keep moving, or, as I like to say, "Go fast and the wrinkles don't show."

11. Do your best every day, and if you can't do your best one day, then do better tomorrow. If you can't remember the first ten rules, then just remembering this one will send you on your way to success in life.

One More Recipe

Since my kids long ago divided my recipes into two categories—brown things and green things—I can't claim to be much of a cook. The fact is that I do have one good recipe in me: a recipe that was given to me over fifty years ago by a cousin of Neal's, and it has never let me down. Since you were kind enough to buy this book, the least I could do for you is pass along my recipe for—what else—apple pie. I confess to having an ulterior motive. If you eat enough of these, then you may need to buy yourself some new clothes. I just happen to have a suggested brand you should buy.

Gert's Finger Apple Pie

INGREDIENTS

Homemade or purchased pie pastry
   for a 9-inch double crust
6 or 7 Granny Smith apples
1 tablespoon fresh lemon juice
½ teaspoon ground cinnamon

½ teaspoon ground allspice

½ teaspoon ground ginger

½ teaspoon ground cloves

¾ cup granulated sugar

¾ cup loosely packed light brown sugar

1 cup slivered almonds (4 ounces)

½ cup or more raisins or golden raisins (optional)

½ cup powdered sugar

About 1 tablespoon water

Roll out the bottom portion of pastry to fit an 11 X 7 X 2-inch baking pan. Roll out the top crust. Cover both crusts with plastic wrap and chill until ready to use.

Peel, core, and thinly slice the apples to make about 5 cups. In a large bowl, toss them gently with the lemon juice, then with the cinnamon, allspice, ginger, and cloves. Toss with granulated sugar, brown sugar, almonds, and raisins.

Preheat oven to 425 degrees.

Remove the pastry-lined pan from the refrigerator.

Spoon in the apple filling and arrange it evenly throughout the pan. Remove the top crust from the refrigerator and unfold it over the filling. Trim the overhangs to 1 inch. Use water to moisten the edges of the crusts where they meet, then press together lightly and turn under. Crimp the edge.

Put the pan on a baking sheet and place the baking sheet on the center rack of the oven. Bake for 10 minutes, then reduce the heat to 350 degrees and bake for 35–45 minutes until the apples are tender, the juices are bubbly, and the crust is golden brown.

Meanwhile, mix the powdered sugar with the water to make a thin paste. Pour or brush over the top crust to make a glaze. Let the pie cool on a rack before cutting into finger-size squares and serving slightly warm or at room temperature. (After you serve the first few pieces, put it in the refrigerator. I like to be able to snitch a piece whenever I feel like it.)

Pin the Tagline on Gert

With each passing year, I think our advertising experts will finally run out of one-liners about my age, my looks, and my charm. And with each passing year, they prove me wrong. I figure if you can't beat 'em, you should join 'em. For example, when I recently traveled to Kentucky for the opening ceremony of a new distribution facility, I announced to the audience—which included the governor of Kentucky—that in honor of our presence in the thoroughbred capital of the world, my nickname was no longer "Tough Mother." Instead, I asked them to call me, "The Old Gray Mare."

Here is a list of some of the taglines that have either accompanied or were proposed to accompany the most unflattering photograph of me possible in Columbia's advertisements. We call them "Gert-isms." If these put you in the spirit to write a "Gert-ism," go ahead and send it to me. You may get a ski jacket in return. Then again, if it's too insulting, I may come over and give you a piece of my mind!

1. If you want something that mellows with age,
   drink wine.

2. The only thing fouler than the weather.

3. Obsessive, anal, fanatical. And that's on a good day.

4. The one thing more bitter than the cold.

5. When you've seen one ice age, you've seen them all.

6. She'll warm everything but your heart.

7. A face only an outdoorsman could love.

8. The original ice queen.

9. She rules with an iron, somewhat wrinkled fist.

10. Rumors persist that Grandmas are kind and gentle.

11. Seasons change. Unfortunately, she doesn't.

12. Blue hair? Maybe. Blue toes? Never.

13. There was an old lady who lived for a shoe.

14. I've got hot flashes to keep me warm.
    You'll need something that zips.

15. What's tough, breathes, and is rather cheap?
    No, not Mother Boyle.

16. Two things I refuse to read: Obituaries and
    weather forecasts.

SPECIAL OLYMPICS

The Mission of Special Olympics

The mission of Special Olympics is to provide year-round sports training and athletic competition in a variety of Olympic-type sports for children and adults with intellectual disabilities, giving them continuing opportunities to develop physical fitness, demonstrate courage, experience joy, and participate in a sharing of gifts, skills, and friendship with their families, other Special Olympic athletes, and the community. There is no charge to participate in Special Olympics. Special Olympics currently serves almost 1.4 million persons with intellectual disabilities in more than 150 countries.

The Philosophy of Special Olympics

Special Olympics is founded on the belief that people with intellectual disabilities can, with proper instruction and encouragement, learn, enjoy, and benefit from participation in individual and team sports.

Special Olympics believes that consistent training is essential to the development of sports skills, and that competition among those of equal abilities is the most appropriate means for testing these skills, measuring progress, and providing incentives for personal growth.

Special Olympics believes that through sports training and competition, people with intellectual disabilities benefit physically, mentally, socially, and spiritually; families are strengthened; and the community at large, both through participation and observation, is united in understanding people with intellectual disabilities in an environment of equality, respect, and acceptance.

The Vision of Special Olympics

Special Olympics is an unprecedented global movement which, through quality sports training and competition, improves the lives of people with intellectual disabilities and, in turn, the lives of everyone they touch.

Special Olympics empowers people with intellectual disabilities to realize their full potential and develop their skills through year-round sports training and competition.

As a result, Special Olympic athletes become fulfilled and productive members of their families and the communities in which they live.

Special Olympics is an experience that is energizing, healthy, welcoming, and joyful.

To the greatest extent possible, Special Olympics activities are run by and involve local volunteers, from school- and college-age individuals to senior citizens, in order to create greater opportunities for public understanding of intellectual disabilities.

For further information or to get involved contact your local Special Olympics Program. To locate a Program near you, go to specialolympics.org.

CASA

*We are advocates for the best interests of children
who have been abused or neglected
and are under the protection of the Juvenile Court.
Our purpose is to secure a safe and permanent family
for each child as quickly as possible.*

*We dedicate our resources to recruiting, training and
supporting citizen volunteers in order to provide
quality advocacy to as many children as we can.*

A Child's Voice in Court®

Each year, thousands of children in our community become wards
of the juvenile court system because they have been victims of
abuse and neglect. While many of these children remain at home
while efforts are made to provide safety, others are placed in foster
or other substitute care placements. Due to complex home
situations and lack of resources, some children can spend years
in foster care until they are reunited with their birth families, or
placed in an adoptive home. Oregon's child welfare system can
only devote so much time and attention to each individual case.
That's where CASA—and maybe you—come in.

Court Appointed Special Advocates are ordinary men and
women from all walks of life, educational levels and ethnic
backgrounds who volunteer to serve as an advocate for a child or
sibling group. Each volunteer commits to 10-20 hours per month
over a 1½ to 2-year period of service. As a result of training and
regular program supervision, CASAs bring objectivity, competence,

tenacity and consistent advocacy into an overloaded child welfare system.

When a CASA volunteer is court-appointed to a case, he or she is responsible for gathering information, and coordinating as many elements as possible, in order to secure for each child a safe, permanent home as quickly as possible. CASAs visit children regularly, review records, interview parents and relatives, consult with teachers, neighbors and foster care providers, and work closely with community service providers. They advocate for the children and families to gain access to needed support and services. They appear in court to advocate on behalf of the child's needs and best interests.

CASAs are an essential and often singularly impactful presence that remind everyone involved—from parents and caseworkers to lawyers and judges—that, at the heart of each case, is a child who deserves a safe and loving place to call home.

CASA for Children is a 501c(3) not-for-profit organization advocating for abused children under the protection of the Juvenile Courts in Multnomah and Washington counties in Oregon. Mandated to exist by the Oregon Legislature in 1985, CASA volunteers are instrumental in turning around the lives of thousands of "at-risk" children.

For more information about CASA for Children, please contact us at (503) 988-5115 or visit our web site at www.casahelpskids.org.

For information about volunteer opportunities at CASA programs nationwide, contact the National CASA Association at (800) 628-3233 or visit www.nationalcasa.org.